DON'T LET

THE

PASTOR CURSE YOU

By Dr. Sheila Hayford

Book Title: Don't Let The Pastor Curse You

Subtitle: - And Neither Should You

Copyright © 2011 by Sheila Hayford, What A Word Publishing and Media Group

ISBN: 978-0-9914039-4-3

Printed in the United States of America.

DEDICATION

This book is dedicated to:

- God the Holy Spirit; my Instructor, my Advisor and
The Revealer of all Truth

- Dr. Ben Carson, whom I first met when I was working
at the Johns Hopkins Hospital in Baltimore, Maryland
and whom I have followed
over the years. Dr. Ben Carson has emerged from
the soft spoken, extremely talented Neurosurgeon I
would strain to hear speak at Grand Rounds to become
one of the strong vocal voices upholding
God's moral authority in the nation

- and to all who have stood up to declare God's truth to man

Sheila Hayford

BOOK REVIEW

The manuscript discusses a wide range of Biblical ideas stretching from the original sin, disobedience, arrogance and remaining connected to God... The author explores various biblical themes with accuracy and passion. The reading includes a variety of illustrative Bible verses, as well as relatable author commentary readers can connect to. Chapter sizes are congruent to each other, creating a streamlined appearance in the text. Readers will find the content is well balanced. The conclusion creates a strong ending for the book that is concise and complete.

Editorial Review.

TABLE OF CONTENTS

Dedication …………………………………………………………..3

Introduction ……………………………………………………6

Authority - Who has it? ………………………………………..8

The Curse of Arrogance …………………………………….16

Do what God Says ……………………………………………24

The Curse of Disobedience ………………………………….31

The Power of Words …………………………………………...37

The Curse of Agreement ……………………………………44

The Curse of Indifference …………………………………...48

The Curse of Displacement ………………………………….53

Epilogue ………………………………………………………58

"Call to Action" Worksheets ………………………………...60

Meet the Author ……………………………………………...94

INTRODUCTION

This book is about Right Thinking, Right Speaking and Right Living. I wrote this book under a mandate from God, for service in and to advance God's kingdom. As such, this book is not intended to be a Pastor bashing book for I recognize the gift God gave us in Pastors and Church leaders. I love my Pastor dearly and have collaborated with many Pastors on various projects. In fact, I would not want to be in the position of speaking against a position that God instituted. Proverbs Chapter 4, verse 7, tells us that wisdom is the principal thing and advises us to get wisdom, and with that understanding. The Bible also warns us in the book of Acts Chapter 17, verse 30, that the times of ignorance God overlooked but now God is commanding all people to repent. There are some things taking place within the church that are not necessarily within the will of God and in the process many are suffering under various curses.

When faced with various challenges and tough circumstances, the natural inclination is to ask "Why?" No doubt the Apostle Paul was asked this question. The Apostle Paul had to explain to the Church in Corinth why some in that church were experiencing various adverse situations. In this book, God gives us an answer to some of the "Why?" questions by opening the eyes of our understanding through the Holy Scriptures. In doing so we are equipped to live more victorious Christian lives. I love that God speaks to the writer as well as those for whom it is written because each one of us has to take personal responsibility for our relationship with God. No one should want to live under a curse when God has provided mankind with the Blessing. And so the question becomes: "Is it really possible to live a curse-free life?" Read on!

By Sheila Hayford.

Write, Write,

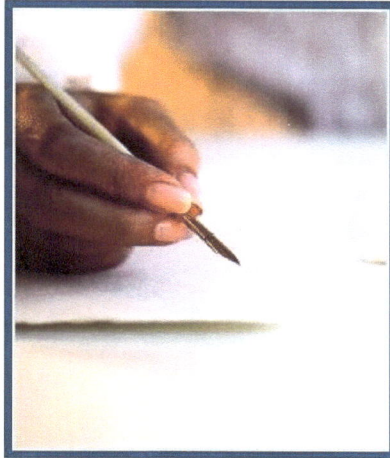

Keep on Writing…

AUTHORITY - WHO HAS IT?

What a great question! We hear the word "Authority" used time and time again. How does Webster's dictionary define it? According to Webster's dictionary authority means: legal or rightful power; a right to command or act; power exercised by a person by virtue of his office or trust; dominion; jurisdiction.

In the book of Matthew Chapter 21, verse 23 of the Holy Bible, the chief priest and the elders of the people came to Jesus, the Christ. "By what authority are you doing these things?" they asked "And who gave you this authority?" In other words, without the proper authority everything that is done is null and void. God understands this. Satan understood this. You should too. So let us establish **proper authority.**

In the book of Genesis Chapter 1, verse 1, we read: "In the beginning God created the heavens and the earth." The first verse in the Bible starts with "In the beginning God created …" This tells us that God is the initiator of all things in the heavens and the earth. More specifically, Authority begins with God. In the book of Genesis Chapter 1 we read that after God had created the heavens and the earth God spoke in verses 26 through verse 30. He said: "Let us make mankind in our image, in our likeness, so that they may rule over the fish in the sea and the birds in the sky, over the livestock and all the wild animals, and over all the creatures that move along the ground. So God created mankind in his own image, in the image of God he created them; male and female he created them. God blessed them and said to them, "Be fruitful and increase in number; fill the earth and subdue it. Rule over the fish in the sea and the birds in the sky and over every living creature that moves on the ground." Then God said, "I give you every seed-bearing plant on the face of the whole earth and every tree that has fruit with seed in it. They will be yours for food. And to all the beasts of the earth and all the birds in the sky and all the creatures that move along the ground - everything that has the breath of life in it - I give every green plant for food." And it was so." **Man was created by God and given territorial dominion or authority by God.**

We must note that God established the boundaries of man's authority. In verses 15 to 17 of the book of Genesis Chapter 2 we read: "The Lord God took the man and put him in the Garden of Eden to take care of it. And the Lord God commanded the man, "You are free to eat from any tree in the garden; but you must not eat from the tree of the knowledge of good and evil, for when you eat from it you will certainly die." In other words, God who had superior authority over man was in a rightful position to give Adam a command. And the God who had created Adam had the authority to decide what to do if Adam did not follow his commands. God also exercised his right or authority to create a woman who would not only help Adam but also relate to Adam as a person. And so God created a woman for Adam whom Adam named Eve. At this time everything was going well between Adam, the woman Eve, and God.

Then satan entered into man's conversation. In the book of Revelation Chapter 12, verses 7 to 9, we read of the insurgency of satan against God. It reads: "Then war broke out in heaven. Michael and his angels fought against the dragon, and the dragon and his angels fought back. But he was not strong enough, and they lost their place in heaven. The great dragon was hurled down - that ancient serpent called the devil, or satan, who leads the whole world astray. He was hurled to the earth, and his angels with him. Michael is an angel of God and satan was originally an angel in the service of God. When satan rebelled against God, satan and the angels who joined satan in the insurgency against God were kicked out of God's palace. God has the power and the authority to punish satan and the rebellious angels in whatever manner God chooses. Satan recognized God's authority and was powerless to stay in possession of the authority satan once had in God's presence. When satan saw Adam and Eve in fellowship with God and the dominion God had given them, satan began to devise another plan against God. But this time satan was going to place man in the midst of his evil plan.

Satan knew God had given man authority in this earth. As a matter of fact, satan was intruding into mankind's territory when he decided to start a conversation with Eve. Satan wanted to be served the way God was, and if he could not get that in God's presence he would try to get that authority in the earth. Remember, God created the earth and gave dominion over the earth to man, for the benefit of mankind, not for satan. Satan knew that in order to get authority in the earth Adam would have to give it to him. Would Adam give up this authority easily? Not if Adam did what God had instructed Adam to do. So satan devised a plan to trick or deceive man. Satan went to Eve, the one closest to Adam and sought an entrance to Adam's authority through Eve. Satan decided to do this by questioning the authority and motive of God's command. In the first place, satan had no business speaking to Eve; he was not in a rightful position to do so. So how did satan pull this off? Satan tried to create doubt and thus contradict the Words of God. And satan suggested that God wanted to hide the knowledge of good and evil from Adam when God gave mankind instructions in the Garden of Eden. Even if God wanted to hide the knowledge of evil from Adam it would be for Adam and Eve's protection. God had placed them in a perfect Garden, they were in perfect relationship with God and they did not need to be exposed to any evil. **Their right relationship with God provided them with the safety, protection and provision they needed.**

Eve would have done well if she had just moved away from satan when satan began talking to her. Instead Eve began to engage in a conversation with satan and was tempted to eat of the fruit of the forbidden tree. And so Eve walked to the tree that God had expressly forbidden man to eat of. In the book of Genesis Chapter 2, verses 16 and 17, it reads: "And the Lord God commanded the man, "You are free to eat from any tree in the garden; but you must not eat from the tree of the knowledge of good and evil, for when you eat from it you will certainly die." Note the sequence of events. First, Eve is distracted when satan starts a conversation with her. Then she fails to walk away when she is tempted by satan. And then she moves in rebellion to God by going to the tree from which God had forbidden man to eat. Finally, Eve plucked a fruit from the tree of which God had forbidden man to eat and ate of it. By eating of that fruit, Eve had now sinned against God. But look at what she did next. She tempted Adam to fall into sin with her. If Eve was going to die as punishment for sinning against God she did not want to die alone. Eve gave a piece of the fruit to Adam and Adam ate of that fruit also. You have to wonder if Adam was in the vicinity when Eve started talking to satan and if so, why he did not ask Eve to leave the presence of satan. And, since Adam knew what God had said concerning the forbidden tree, why did Adam choose to yield to the temptation of Eve? Just like that, Adam and Eve had sinned against God by yielding to the temptation of satan instead of obeying the command of God. And so it was that Adam and Eve birthed sin into the human race. Mankind had now sinned against God by yielding to satan's temptation and in so doing had also transferred the authority God had given mankind over to satan. **For you see, the one whose advice you listen to and follow is the one you have willingly given control or authority over you or what you are doing.** And with that Adam and Eve brought the curse of sin on all humanity. God pronounced the punishment for this sin and as a result satan was cursed, Adam, Eve and all humanity was cursed, and the earth was cursed. Remember this. Adam and Eve sinned when they obeyed satan instead of obeying God; but in addition to the curse that came upon Adam and

Eve as a result of their sin, the ground of the earth was also cursed. **In other words, when Adam and Eve disobeyed God, Adam and Eve were cursed and the realm of Adam and Eve's dominion was also cursed.**

But this is not the end of the story. God would not be God if he did not know that this would happen. So God brought the Lord Jesus Christ into the picture. Yes, mankind had now sinned against God. Adam and Eve no longer had moral and physical authority in the earth and what was in the earth was now under the authority of satan. What would the Lord Jesus Christ do to change this? First, Jesus would be born of a woman, the legal way to enter the earth. In other words he would come as God the Son in the flesh, live a life without sin and then carry the penalty for sin in his body on behalf of Adam, Eve and all mankind. In the gospel of Matthew Chapter 4, verses 8 to 11, satan tries to circumvent this mission by asking the Lord Jesus Christ to bow down and worship satan in exchange for the kingdoms of the world. It reads: "Again, the devil took him to a very high mountain and showed him all the kingdoms of the world and their splendor. "All this I will give you," he said, "if you will bow down and worship me." Jesus said to him, "Away from me, Satan! For it is written: Worship the Lord your God, and serve him only." Then the devil left him, and angels came and attended him." When satan spoke those words to tempt the Lord Jesus, satan understood that he now had the authority Adam had transferred to satan regarding dominion in this earth. However, the Lord Jesus, who was present at the time of creation, refused to yield to satan's temptation and refused to circumvent or abort God's assignment for his life. The Lord Jesus continued to live a life on this earth without committing any sin.

When the Lord Jesus died on the cross for the sins of all mankind and rose up triumphantly from the dead, Jesus Christ took back the authority of this earth from satan and made it possible for every human being to once again enter into a right relationship with God. Thus, the Lord Jesus made it possible for every person to exert his or her God given dominion in this earth. Listen to the words of our Lord Jesus in the gospel of Luke Chapter 10, verses 17 through 20: "The seventy-two returned with joy and said, "Lord, even the demons submit to us in your name. He replied, "I saw Satan fall like lightning from heaven. I have given you authority to trample on snakes and scorpions and to overcome all the power of the enemy; nothing will harm you. However, do not rejoice that the spirits submit to you, but rejoice that your names are written in heaven."

You might ask: What has this got to do with the Pastor? Everything! You see, in the book of Ephesians Chapter 4, verse 11, we understand that Pastors are one of the gifts the Lord Jesus Christ has given to the church. And we learned from Adam that if a person is cursed, the territory under their dominion is adversely affected. If a Pastor has chosen to live a life that is outside God's will by living outside the stated will and Words of God they will experience God's judgment and those under the Pastor's authority may be affected. In 2nd Samuel Chapter 24, King David disobeyed God by counting the army even though Joab and the army commanders had told him not to. As a result of King David's disobedience, God sent a plague to the land and many people under King David's jurisdiction were affected by that plague.

In the book of 2nd Kings Chapter 1, King Ahaziah sent a captain and fifty men to bring the prophet Elijah to the king. The captain and the messengers were obeying the king's command because they were under the king's authority and had consented to his order, whether the order was good or bad. Nonetheless, when the prophet Elijah spoke against the messengers who had been sent by King Ahaziah, all those messengers were immediately killed. When you agree to become a member of a local church fellowship, you place yourself under the leaders in that church fellowship voluntarily. And if the Pastor lives a life of sexual immorality, or preaches a message that is in open rebellion to the Word of God, the congregation under their leadership is adversely affected.

While the Lord Jesus Christ has made the way for the redemption of mankind possible, it is not automatic. A person has to first recognize and admit that they have sinned against God and therefore deserve God's punishment of death and judgment. The person has to accept the fact that the Lord Jesus Christ has paid the price or judgment for their sin. They must confess their sins to God and ask for forgiveness through Jesus Christ. The person must also willingly accept the Lord Jesus Christ as their personal Lord and Savior. **In other words, that person gives the Lord Jesus Christ full authority in every aspect of their life.** All who receive the Lord Jesus Christ as their personal Savior and Lord are now born again as explained by the Lord Jesus Christ in the gospel of John; this second birth is into the kingdom of God. They are moved from satan's kingdom of darkness into the family of God. All who receive the Lord Jesus Christ into their heart become children of God and joint heirs with Christ EQUALLY. In other words **the righteous standing we receive from the Lord Jesus Christ at the time of salvation is equal for every person of the human race.** Pastors and Church leaders are given positions in the church to build up the church and to equip the members in and for God's service. It is very important that we respect the position of the Pastor or Church leader but not be intimidated by it. Why?

Because each Pastor or church leader is a human being and like all human beings has to face the challenges and the limitations of his or her humanity. Yes, God will use the Pastor or Church leader to speak, preach and have oversight of those under their leadership. But each Church leader should be constantly growing in their relationship with God and in their understanding of God's Word. What a Pastor or Church leader thought today was "sound Doctrine" based on his or her Christian maturity and understanding of God's Word may not be the same understanding they have five years after they preached a particular sermon. The Apostle Paul in the book of 1st Timothy Chapter 3 gives the qualifications he expects of a church leader. And he warns us in verse 6 of the same Chapter not to have a novice or an immature Christian as a church leader. Moreover, in the book of Acts Chapter 17, verses 10 and 11, Paul commends the Berean Christians for checking out what their church leaders told them to see if it was so. You might not be around to hear the Pastor explain his more mature position based on better revelation of the solid Word of God later in his or her life. That is why it is important to not only pray for our church leaders, but also to spend time reading and studying the Holy Bible ourselves. That way we grow in our relationship with God and in our understanding of how God wants us to live.

If a person, therefore, willingly places themselves under the leadership of one who is in open rebellion to the commands, ways and precepts of God, that person has willingly placed themselves under a curse.

Pharaoh, the King of Egypt in the book of Genesis Chapter 12, verses 9 to 20, was in grave trouble with God because he placed Abram's wife, Sarah, under Pharaoh's authority. He did so when he took Sarah from Abram and placed her in Pharaoh's house. God brought upon Pharaoh and Pharaoh's house great plagues because of Sarah. In all fairness, Abram did not tell the king the whole truth when he said that Sarah was his sister, but that did not stop the curse from falling on Pharaoh and Pharaoh's house. When Pharaoh recognized that Sarah was Abram's wife he was obviously upset with Abram and wisely sent Abram and Sarah away.

As a child of God, or a member of a church fellowship, you have the responsibility of studying God's Word for yourself. We should not neglect fellowshipping with other believers. At the same time you cannot depend on your church leader or Pastor to give you one hundred percent of all the Scriptures you will ever read or study. The Pastor has a personal responsibility towards God and towards you. You have a personal responsibility towards God and towards your church leaders. You have the God given authority to live a victorious Christian life that should be enhanced when you fellowship with others. And it should be at a place where the Word of God is preached uncompromisingly. As a child, you were under your parent's instructions and you had to obey them in their choice of a church fellowship, but as an adult no one should force you to belong to a particular church fellowship. It may have been your great grandfather's church fellowship but that does not necessarily make it the place where you should fellowship. God has the ultimate authority over your life, not a person. We pray to receive the Lord Jesus Christ as our personal Lord and Savior when we accept responsibility for our sins and accept the gift of salvation through the Lord Jesus Christ who took the punishment for our sins. This brings us into right standing with God and we are born again into the family of God. In the gospel of John Chapter 1, verses 12 and 13, we read: "Yet to all who did receive him, to those who believed in his name, he gave the right to become children of God - children born not of natural descent, nor of human decision or a husband's will, but born of God." We must also pray and ask God, with counsel from God's Word and God the Holy Spirit, where we should choose our home church fellowship, recognizing the power of Authority. And then we must apply the wisdom of God and make the right decision. Don't let the Pastor curse you. Neither should you, directly or indirectly, wittingly or unwittingly curse yourself.

Write, Write,

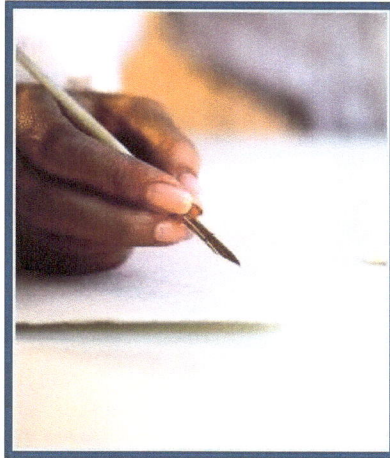

Keep on Writing…

THE CURSE OF ARROGANCE

I heard a Pastor tell the congregation that they would never rise above the spiritual level of the Pastor. At the time I knew he was wrong and now I would say that statement was an arrogant one. Why? It is because that presumed that the Pastor was providing one hundred percent of the spiritual instruction needed for each individual member of the church. Such a statement gives no room for personal independent Christian study and growth and limit's the work of the Holy Spirit in those who follow that concept or philosophy. **You see, church fellowship attendance should not be the totality of a person's Christian experience. God wants us to have personal time with Him too.**

The Pastor obviously has a responsibility to teach and preach the Word of God. The Pastor also has a responsibility to counsel, correct, and to lead, under God's direction, the affairs in the church. The Pastor must take time to hear from God and share what God would have him or her say to the church. He or she should seek the wellbeing of themselves and the members of the congregation. At the same time consider this. God would not be fair if God limited your Christian faith and your walk with God to the spiritual level of your Pastor. And if you changed the church where you fellowshipped at or visited another church you would be in yo-yo mode, limited to the ups and downs of whichever Pastor was providing leadership in the church you attended. **By limiting God in such a manner an individual would be limiting their fullest potential in God.** <u>Not only that, the individual would be placing themselves under the curse of putting their Christian walk, growth and trust entirely in the hands of another human being instead of fully trusting in the ability of the Holy Spirit to lead and mature them.</u> God is always speaking to us; in His Word, directly and through others, through various media such as radio and television and even in the beauty of His creation. Should we love our Pastor and church leaders in general? Of course! Should we appreciate our Pastors? Very much so! And should we give our Pastors the freedom to be who they really are, persons who are walking out the call of God even as they face the challenges of their position and the limitations of their humanity? Yes. You see, Pastors get discouraged and sometimes feel like giving up. Pastors are tempted, maybe in different areas than some. The Lord Jesus Christ had to deal with the temptations satan tried to bring Him and the challenges of living in this earth realm and He gave us the greatest example of how we should live life in this world. The Lord Jesus is the only one who lived a sinless life here on earth and by the power of the Holy Spirit we can each live a victorious Christian life regardless of what another person may or may not be doing. We should not minimize the role of the Pastor; at the same time, we should not overextend that role.

Arrogance may also express itself subtly. We hear the expressions "my church" or "my congregation" used all the time. But think about this. Is it really my church? Is it really the Pastor's church? **Or is it the church of the Lord Jesus Christ since it is the Lord Jesus Christ who died to save mankind?** And that is where the subtle potential for denominations to become a curse to their members lies. We sometimes hear statements like "in my church the women have to cover their heads", or "women are not allowed to preach in our denomination", or "in our denomination we attend church on Saturdays and not on Sundays". In other words, many are focused on the differences that, unrelated to salvation through Jesus Christ, cause division in the global church of the Lord Jesus Christ, instead of uniting to fight satan, who is the common enemy. We must share the good news of salvation through the Lord Jesus Christ with those who are walking in slavation* to satan. Remember the words of the Lord Jesus Christ in the gospel of Matthew Chapter 12, verse 25 when he said a house divided against itself cannot stand. In James Chapter 3, verse 16 we are told that where envy and strife exists there is every evil work. The reason the church has not made a greater impact on the lives of our communities is partly because of the infighting amongst those who say they are Christians.

Have you heard a Pastor or Church leader tell the members of the congregation that they cannot attend another church without the Pastor's permission? I understand that when you are in a position of leadership or responsibility in a church you have the responsibility of showing up in church and on time, whether it is on a Sunday or whatever days you have made the commitment to do so. That is a part of being faithful to your assignment. However, if a member of a church fellowship wishes to visit another church fellowship for a special event such as a child christening, should that member have to get permission from the Pastor to do so? It would obviously be nice to let someone at your church fellowship know you will not be in attendance at your church home fellowship that day so the congregation is not worried about your wellbeing. However, a member should not be made to feel guilty for fellowshipping with another part of the body of Christ without first getting the Pastor's permission.

Many people who attend church do so after they have made the decision to receive the Lord Jesus Christ into their life as their personal Lord and Savior. There are also many who come to church in the process of searching for God or who are young in their Christian experience and are looking for answers and meaning to the circumstances in their lives. **We must not place ungodly limitations on people where God has granted freedom.**

Let's look at something as basic as food, and more specifically the issue of eating pork or meat. In the book of Acts Chapter 10, verses 9 to 16 in the King James translation, the Apostle Peter describes a vision given to him by the Lord God. Peter was hungry and wanted to eat. While the food was being made ready, Peter saw an object that looked like a sheet tied at the four ends with all kinds of creatures in it; four footed animals, wild animals, creeping things and birds of the air. Then he heard a voice telling him: "Rise, Peter; kill and eat." In the Jewish practice in the Old Testament they did not eat pork and so Peter gave this reply: "Not so, Lord; for I have never eaten anything common or unclean." Listen to what God said in reply: "What God has cleansed you must not call common." The Bible tells us that this was done three times and I believe this was done three times for emphasis because the Holy Spirit knew many would still be having this conversation today. You see, the first Adam drove mankind into sin. The last Adam, as the Lord Jesus Christ is referred to in the book of 1st Corinthians Chapter 15, verse 45, redeemed mankind from sin and restored mankind back to our rightful dominion. And that authority and dominion through the Lord Jesus Christ is true for born again believers throughout the ages. So what should one do if a born again believer feels it is against his conscience at the time to eat pork or meat? Should he or she be forced to eat pork just because another person walks in their liberty in Christ to eat whatever food they want? No! Neither should the person who does not want to eat pork despise, intimidate or try to coerce those who eat pork or meat to abstain from such food.

Listen to the words of the Apostle Paul in the book of Romans Chapter 14, verses 1 through 23. It reads: **"Accept the one whose faith is weak, without quarreling over disputable matters. One person's faith allows them to eat anything, but another, whose faith is weak, eats only vegetables. The one who eats everything must not treat with contempt the one who does not, and the one who does not eat everything must not judge the one who does, for God has accepted them. Who are you to judge someone else's servant? To their own master, servants stand or fall. And they will stand, for the Lord is able to make them stand.** One person considers one day more sacred than another; another considers every day alike. Each of them should be fully convinced in their own mind. Whoever regards one day as special does so to the Lord. Whoever eats meat does so to the Lord, for they give thanks to God; and whoever abstains does so to the Lord and gives thanks to God. For none of us lives for ourselves alone, and none of us dies for ourselves alone. If we live, we live for the Lord; and if we die, we die for the Lord. So, whether we live or die, we belong to the Lord. For this very reason, Christ died and returned to life so that he might be the Lord of both the dead and the living. You, then, why do you judge your brother or sister? Or why do you treat them with contempt? For we will all stand before God's judgment seat. It is written: 'As surely as I live,' says the Lord, 'every knee will bow before me; every tongue will acknowledge God'. So then, each of us will give an account of ourselves to God. Therefore let us stop passing judgment on one another. Instead, make up your mind not to put any stumbling block or obstacle in the way of a brother or sister. **I am convinced, being fully persuaded in the Lord Jesus, that nothing is unclean in itself. But if anyone regards something as unclean, then for that person it is unclean. If your brother or sister is distressed because of what you eat, you are no longer acting in love. Do not by your eating destroy someone for whom Christ died. Therefore do not let what you know is good be spoken of as evil. For the kingdom of God is not a matter of eating and drinking, but of righteousness, peace and joy in the Holy Spirit**, anyone who serves Christ in this way is pleasing to God and receives human approval. Let us therefore make every effort to do what leads to peace and to mutual edification. Do not destroy the work of God for the sake of food. All food is clean, but it is wrong for a person to eat anything that causes someone else to stumble. It is better not to eat meat or drink wine or to do anything else that will cause your brother or sister to fall. So whatever you believe about these things keep between yourself and God. **Blessed is the one who does not condemn himself by what he approves. But whoever has doubts is condemned if they eat, because their eating is not from faith; and everything that does not come from faith is sin.**" In all things, love for our fellow believer should be a great motivator. <u>We should enjoy the freedom that the Lord Jesus Christ gives us and yet take into consideration the faith and conscience of another believer.</u> If eating pork in the presence of a believer who feels it is not right will cause your fellow believer to stumble, enjoy your pork at home.

Heed the words of the prophet Micah in the book of Micah Chapter 3, verses 5 to 12: "This is what the Lord says: "As for the prophets who lead my people astray, they proclaim 'peace' if they have something to eat, but prepare to wage war against anyone who refuses to feed them. Therefore night will come over you, without visions, and darkness, without divination. The sun will set for the prophets, and the day will go dark for them. The seers will be ashamed and the diviners disgraced. They will all cover their faces because there is no answer from God." But as for me, I am filled with power, with the Spirit of the Lord, and with justice and might, to declare to Jacob his transgression, to Israel his sin. Hear this, you leaders of Jacob, you rulers of Israel, who despise justice and distort all that is right; who build Zion with bloodshed, and Jerusalem with wickedness. Her leaders judge for a bribe, her priests teach for a price, and her prophets tell fortunes for money. Yet they look for the Lord's support and say, "Is not the Lord among us? No disaster will come upon us." Therefore because of you, Zion will be plowed like a field, Jerusalem will become a heap of rubble," In these days of political correctness and in some cases, an overemphasis of financial wealth as a testament of God's favor, some Pastors and Church leaders will not take up a speaking engagement if the inviting group does not guarantee $10,000.00 or more in advance payment for that speaking engagement. Some in church ministry will not pray over a prayer request if the mailed envelope did not include a contribution to that ministry. Is that the example the Lord Jesus gave us? True, the Lord Jesus tells us in the gospel of Luke Chapter 10, verse 7 that "the worker deserves his wages" and if you invite a Pastor or Church leader to minister at a particular fellowship it is certainly expected that you will do your best to make that person comfortable so that Pastor or Church leader is free to focus on the Word God has for him or her to share with the congregation. However, there may be something wrong if the Pastor or Church leader demands that a limousine picks him or her from the airport for a speaking engagement when the members of that congregation cannot afford to pay for a limousine and could have a trusted member of the congregation provide that ride. It maybe that God asked the congregation to invite the Pastor because God was setting the Pastor up for a blessing; a blessing based on God's terms. You see, the book of Proverbs Chapter 19, verse 17 tells us that whoever is kind to the poor, that is, to those who cannot afford to directly pay them back, lends to the Lord God. And I can say that God knows how to pay a person back really good, naturally and supernaturally, without that person demanding burdensome or offensive obligations of others.

In the book of Daniel Chapter 5, we read about the arrogance of King Belshazzar, a man who God had placed in a position of authority. He was the son of King Nebuchadnezzar, the king God brought down when he became prideful. We read in the book of Daniel that King Nebuchadnezzar was driven by God to live among animals, eating grass until he was ready to acknowledge God's authority and dominion. Nebuchadnezzar's son, King Belshazzar, had a great feast and invited several of the lords. At this event he commanded that the sacred golden and silver vessels that were taken from the temple at Jerusalem be brought to the feast so that King Belshazzar, his wives and concubines, as well as the princes in the land would drink wine from these vessels. How arrogant! That was in flagrant disregard to God's commandments. So what happened to King Belshazzar? The curse of arrogance showed up in the form of the handwriting on the wall. And this was no ordinary handwriting. It was the fingers of the hand sent from God and they wrote the curse from God upon King Belshazzar. King Belshazzar's reign would end because God had examined the king and found him wanting, or failing the test. That night, King Belshazzar was killed.

In modern days we may not see a king asking that communion vessels be brought out of the church to a royal or state dinner. However, arrogance may present itself more subtly. God is not mocked when people ridicule the principles and precepts God has placed in the Holy Bible and begin to give their own interpretations of what God calls sin. Just like satan they start out with "Hath God said…" and then try to justify why they think God does not have their wellbeing at the heart of God's command. In Chapter 32 of the book of Exodus we read that when the prophet Moses was on the mount with God, the priest Aaron who was assigned by God to help Moses yielded to the wishes of the people and asked the people to bring their gold. Aaron then created a golden calf image for the people to worship. Aaron, as a priest, knew the commandments of God in Exodus Chapter 20 when God told the people of Israel not to build for themselves any graven images nor to bow down or worship those images. However, Aaron yielded to the pressure of those who wanted to rebel against God's commands. As a result of their disobedience to God's commands, about three thousand men died and the casualty would have been higher if Moses had not personally interceded with God on behalf of the people.

Thank God for the Lord Jesus Christ. Almost every one of us has at one time or other said or done things out of arrogance or pride. What should we do? Is there hope for forgiveness from a holy God? Of course there is. In the book of Romans we see that if we are truly sorry and confess our sins before God, whatever that sin may be, we can receive forgiveness from God. God will forgive us because of the death, burial and resurrection of the Lord Jesus Christ on behalf of our sins. You see, there is a difference between guilt and conviction. If we sin, God the Holy Spirit convicts us of the sin and points us to the Lord Jesus Christ to whom we can turn for forgiveness. However, if a person experiences guilt as a result of their sin but is too arrogant or prideful to repent of their sin, confess their sin to God and ask for God's forgiveness, they are condemned to the punishment of God for their sins. This is because they have refused or rejected God's way of salvation and forgiveness through the Lord Jesus Christ.

* Not a typographical error. I made up the word "slavation" for emphasis on what satan really does to a person when they are under the power of satan to contrast that with salvation through Jesus Christ.

Write, Write,

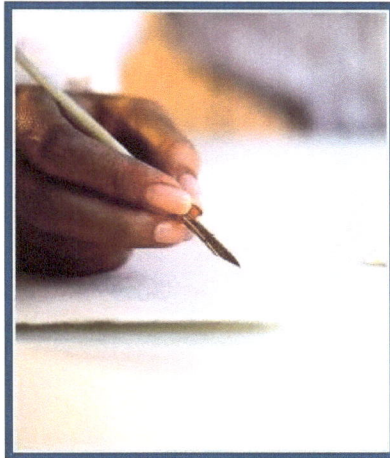

Keep on Writing…

DO WHAT GOD SAYS

In the gospel of John Chapter 14, verse 15, the Lord Jesus Christ gives us a litmus test to demonstrate our love for him. The Lord Jesus tells us that if we love him we will keep his commandments. **How many times do we tell God, ourselves and others that we love God? If we really love God, then we must keep God's commandments. In other words, we must do what God says.** So what does God command us to do? God gives us general commands, specific commands and personal commands.

First, there are the **general commands** that God gives to mankind. Examples of these are found in the book of Exodus Chapter 20, verses 1 through 17, and are referred to as the Ten Commandments. It reads: "And God spoke all these words: "I am the Lord your God, who brought you out of Egypt, out of the land of slavery. You shall have no other gods before me. "You shall not make for yourself an image in the form of anything in heaven above or on the earth beneath or in the waters below. You shall not bow down to them or worship them; for I, the Lord your God, am a jealous God, punishing the children for the sin of the parents to the third and fourth generation of those who hate me, but showing love to a thousand generations of those who love me and keep my commandments. "You shall not misuse the name of the Lord your God, for the Lord will not hold anyone guiltless who misuses his name." Remember the Sabbath day by keeping it holy. Six days you shall labor and do all your work, but the seventh day is a sabbath to the Lord your God. On it you shall not do any work, neither you, nor your son or daughter, nor your male or female servant, nor your animals, nor any foreigner residing in your towns. For in six days the Lord made the heavens and the earth, the sea, and all that is in them, but he rested on the seventh day. Therefore the Lord blessed the Sabbath day and made it holy. "Honor your father and your mother, so that you may live long in the land the Lord your God is giving you." You shall not murder. "You shall not commit adultery." You shall not steal. "You shall not give false testimony against your neighbor." You shall not covet your neighbor's house. You shall not covet your neighbor's wife, or his male or female servant, his ox or donkey, or anything that belongs to your neighbor."

The Lord Jesus summarized the Ten Commandments in the book of Matthew Chapter 22, verses 37 to 40, when he said we are to love the Lord God with all our heart, mind and soul and to love our neighbor as ourselves. In Chapter 10 of the book of Luke, we read about an expert of the law who upon hearing this summary asked the Lord Jesus: "And who is my neighbor?" Jesus Christ answered him with the parable of the Good Samaritan in verses 30 to 37 of the same Chapter. The Lord Jesus then told the man to go and do likewise. So we are now without excuse as to who we should love and whose good we should seek. A lot of the evil we see taking place in the world would be avoided if the Ten Commandments were practiced in daily living. A person who chooses to commit adultery is coveting someone that is not legally theirs. Someone covets another person's lifestyle and steals the other person's belongings. Nations have gone to war because they coveted the natural resources of a less powerful people. People have been physically and emotionally hurt just because someone wanted the pair of sneakers they were wearing. And, in Christian circles, people have been slandered because someone coveted the spiritual gifts God had given them. We are responsible to God first for how we live the life God has given us and we must diligently work with the gifts God has given us. God's commandments to mankind are not burdensome. Indeed, the rewards of obedience to God are a much better alternative to the consequences of sin and the punishment of sin by God.

And then there are the specific commands God gives us. In the book of Deuteronomy God gave specific commands to the Israelites. In Deuteronomy Chapter 28, God lists the benefits, rewards or blessings that would come to the people as a result of obeying God's specific commands. This confirms that God gives us commands to follow for our good and not for evil. God tells us in the book of Jeremiah Chapter 29, verse 11: "For I know the plans I have for you," declares the Lord, "plans to prosper you and not to harm you, plans to give you hope and a future." A specific command that the Lord Jesus Christ gives us is found in Matthew Chapter 18, verses 21 and 22 and it is that we forgive those who wrong us. Here the Lord Jesus is essentially telling Peter to forgive every time a person does him wrong. The Lord Jesus tells us in Matthew Chapter 18, verse 7, that offenses will come and warns us against offending others. In other words, there will be opportunities for you to hold a grudge or harbor unforgiveness. God does not release the person causing the offense from their wrong doing because the Lord Jesus says in verse 6 of the same chapter that it would be better for one who offends a child to have a millstone hang on their neck and drowned. **But God in His wisdom knows that forgiveness releases you from the hurt and evil the other person tried to put on you and allows God, and not you, to deal with their punishment.**

And what should you do if you have offended someone? First, confess your sin to God and seek forgiveness from God. God will forgive you if you have truly repented. Then you should go to the person you wronged quickly, admit your wrongdoing and genuinely ask for their forgiveness.

If they forgive you, you have to show them by your future actions that you were truly sorry for what you did to them. If the person you wronged chooses not to forgive you, you should still pray for them and commit the situation and the consequences of your action into the hands of God. The Lord God, through the Holy Scriptures, has specific commands for those who have accepted the Lord Jesus as their Savior and Lord. To those who say they are born again believers and disciples of the Lord Jesus Christ, the Lord Jesus says in the book of John Chapter 13, verse 34: "A new command I give you: Love one another. As I have loved you, so you must love one another." In the book of 1st Corinthians Chapter 13 we are given various attributes of love. The command therefore to us, as believers in the Lord Jesus Christ, is to love fellow believers with the love attributes described in these verses. In evaluating whether we love others the way God would have us love them, we must all ask ourselves if our actions are demonstrating these love attributes. Where we fall short, the Holy Spirit, who is given to every born again believer as a gift from God, is ready and able to help us in our love journey. God loves us and wants us to love others with God's kind of love. God will enable us to share His love with others.

And then there are the **personal commands** God gives to an individual. It is important to note that what may be a personal command from God to you may not necessarily be a personal command from God to me and vice versa. In the book of Genesis Chapter 22 we read that God tested Abraham when he gave Abraham a personal command to offer his son, Isaac, as a sacrifice to God. Abraham was ready to obey God when God gave him another personal command to hold off the sacrifice of Isaac. God birthed each of us into this world with a specific purpose and plan. In other words, God has a unique plan for you that is specifically for you.

Along the way God's plan for you may merge with God's plan for another person or may include God's plan for several people. And that is why it is of paramount importance that each individual learns to hear God speak for themselves. God will not reveal one hundred percent of God's plan for you to the Pastor but God will reveal God's plans for you to you in private, through others and corporately if you are in right relationship with God. And if what God tells you to do conflicts with what another person tells you to do, you must obey God. In the book of 1st Kings Chapter 13, verse 9 the Lord God gave specific commands to a man of God when God told him not to eat any bread or drink water nor return in the same way in which he came on that particular assignment. However, when the sons of the old prophet told the old prophet the works that man of God had done and the personal command the Lord God had given this man of God, the old prophet devised a way to trip this man into disobeying God. We see how he did that in verses 11 to 19 of the same Chapter. The old prophet started out by saying that he too was a prophet of God and that an angel had given him instructions regarding the man of God that contradicted what God had directly told the man of God. Does that sound familiar? Tragically the man followed the old prophet and disobeyed God. But even more 'surprising' is that after the old prophet had caused the man of God to disobey God, the old prophet prophesied God's judgment on the man of God for disobeying God. When the man of God left the old prophet's house after disobeying God when he ate bread and drank water at the old prophet's house, he was killed by a lion and his body left in the street. And guess who picked up the man's body to bury him? In verse 29 of 1st Kings Chapter 13 we are told it was the old prophet!

Be careful not to allow others to cause you to disobey God for they might be the same ones condemning you and saying: "You should have obeyed God!" Which begs the question: "Why didn't they say that earlier?" You see, disobedience to a personal command of God occurred when the young man obeyed the old prophet instead of doing what God had told him to do. This resulted in the untimely death of this man of God, and with that any future work this man might have done. There is certainly wisdom in seeking spiritual guidance and instruction from others. However, there are some things God tells you to do that He does not always reveal to others. Before you dismiss spiritual guidance or instruction it is important to examine yourself, spending time with God and the Word of God, to make sure what you perceive as a personal command from God does not conflict with the truths of the Holy Bible. **And then do what God says.**

In the book of Daniel Chapter 3, King Nebuchadnezzar passed a law that said that the people in the province of Babylon were to bow down before a manmade graven image. That was in direct contradiction to God's commandment in Exodus Chapter 20 and so Shadrach, Meshach and Abednego refused to obey the king's commands. The king was furious with them and threatened to throw them into a burning fiery furnace. They still refused to obey the king and said that if God did not deliver them from the fire they were willing to die for the sake of their faith in God's Word. How many have been told by a leader in the church that if they did not compromise on a particular position or situation, they would not be ordained to or given a specific position in the church? Some have compromised their Christian beliefs and morals because they wanted to remain in the favor of the people in power, even when those leaders had taken stands or positions that were directly opposed to the Word of God. **What should we do when asked to compromise on a general, specific or personal command from God? The answer is to do what God says and stand your Christian ground.** Shadrach, Meshach and Abednego were delivered by God from the fiery furnace without even the smell of fire on them.

Stephen, a man of faith and filled with the Holy Spirit, spoke the truth of God's Word when it was unpopular to do so and in so doing put his life in danger. God allowed Stephen to be stoned to death because, as the book of Hebrews Chapter 11, verses 37 and 38 tells us, the world was not worthy of those martyrs who died as a result of their faith in God. In the long run it is not what the Pastor or others think or say about you that matters; it is what God has to say about you. If you are threatened with the loss of your position or thrown out of the church fellowship for standing up for God's truth, entrust yourself into the powerful hands of God. The Lord God tells us in Romans Chapter 8, verse 28 that He will work all things out for the good of those who love God and who are the called according to the purposes and plans of God.

Is it difficult to do what God says? In a sense, yes and no. Yes, it may be difficult to do what God says because it may conflict with the natural instincts of a person. As a teenager, you may want to obey God and remain sexually pure until marriage even when some in society apply pressure for you to do otherwise. Despite what some may say there are countless Christians, including the famous N.B.A. basketball athlete A.C. Green, who will tell you that being a virgin until marriage can be done. It will, however, take God's help and power to live a holy life. And no, living for God is not really difficult because when you choose to obey God you are empowered by the Holy Spirit and rewarded by God. In the book of Hebrews Chapter 11, verse 6 we see that God not only wants us to believe in Him but to also believe that He is a Rewarder of those who diligently seek Him. Are we perfect as we live life on this earth? No. However, our goal is for God to work in us as He shows others the character and love of the Lord Jesus by the way we live here on earth.

When we obey God in His general commandments we reap general blessings, made possible by our right standing with God through our Lord Jesus Christ. General commands are commands that God gives to all mankind. When we obey God in specific commands, such as those given to the disciples of the Lord Jesus Christ and other specific groups, we reap specific rewards. And when we obey God in the personal individual commands God gives us, we reap individual rewards. The beautiful thing is that those rightly connected to us when we live in obedience to the commands of God may also enjoy God's blessings. In the book of Genesis we see how Joseph obeyed God despite gross injustice. Joseph was later used by God, as we read in Genesis Chapter 47, verses 1 to 11, to greatly help his father and brethren during the time of famine.

Some benefits we experience here on earth, other benefits we will have when we meet our Lord Jesus Christ on the other side of eternity. Remember the words of the Lord Jesus in the book of Revelations Chapter 22, verses 12 to 14: "And, behold I come quickly; and my reward is with me, to give every man according as his work shall be. I am Alpha and Omega, the beginning and the end, the first and the last. Blessed are they that do his commandments, that they may have right to the tree of life, and may enter in through the gates into the city." What a great motivation; enjoying the rewards given to us by our precious Lord Jesus Christ as we spend eternity with Him.

Write, Write,

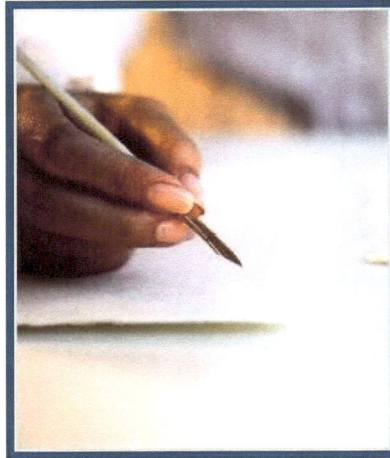

Keep on Writing…

THE CURSE OF DISOBEDIENCE

Just as there are blessings for obeying God's commandments, whether they are general, specific or personal commands, so there are curses for disobeying God's commands. And that is why it is vitally important for church leaders to be careful in the way they live. In Chapter 20 of the book of Exodus, we not only read the Ten Commandments, we also read about some of the curses that come from disobeying these commands. In verse 5 of Exodus Chapter 20, we read that God will punish to the third and fourth generations those who show hatred for God by forsaking God and worshipping other gods. In verse 7 of the same Chapter we read that God will judge as guilty those who take the name of God in vain. Moreover, in the book of Deuteronomy Chapter 28, verses 15 through 68, we read the specific curses that would come upon the Israelites if they disobeyed the specific commands God had given them. In verse 22 of that same Chapter God specified the diseases that would come upon the people as a curse if they disobeyed God's commands. Could it be, therefore, that some are sick because they are under a curse?

I visited a church where several members of the congregation had a specific terminal illness. What was more surprising to me was the general tone of the conversation of the members of that congregation. Each was trying to outdo the other in their physical symptoms, doctor appointments and doctor visits, and seemed oblivious to the fact that a curse was operating in their midst. I did not hear the Pastor call for a period of fasting and praying in the church on behalf of those who needed specific healing for that illness, nor for the casting out of the spirits of infirmity from any in whom such spirits may be operating. Neither did I hear him radically believing God for the healing of the bodies of those affected in authoritative prayer. I was told there was a nurse in the congregation who would give general advice and I wondered I why there was such an emphasis placed on sickness instead of on health. Did I feel compassion towards those suffering with that condition? Yes! Did I want to tell them that they could believe God and see God work healing miracles with and without the limitations of humankind? Yes! I knew that would not be the "home" place of church fellowship and decided not to go back there. Did I think I was superior to those fellowshipping there? Of course not! However, I did not want to have any part of that curse by association! Am I saying all sickness is a result of a curse? In a sense, Yes! That is because when Adam and Eve sinned by disobeying God they no longer had perfect health and thus introduced sin and sickness into humankind. We earlier referenced Deuteronomy Chapter 28 verse 2 where we understand that some sicknesses are a result of direct disobedience to God's commands. However, the book of Job is an example of the fact that not all sickness is a direct result of disobedience to God. We can understand that a healthy lifestyle contributes to good health and an unhealthy lifestyle contributes to poor health. Could God work miracles in that church? Of course! Was I protected by the blood of the Lord Jesus Christ while I was there? Yes, indeed. Could I have told the Pastor what I felt they needed to do in the church? Yes, I could. But that was not my place at the time. I was there to visit and discerned they really were not prepared for my observations. In addition, I perceived they might not even be willing to accept as Biblical God's desire for the healing and health of mankind - past, present and throughout the ages. For you see, if a person is under spiritual leadership where the Pastor or denomination does not believe that the Lord Jesus Christ still heals today, or that the Lord Jesus suffered in Isaiah Chapter 53 the beatings, torture, death, burial and resurrection in order that salvation and healing may come to mankind, or that evil spirits need to be cast out in the authority of and in the Name of the Lord Jesus Christ, then the person who may be afflicted is doomed if they are under a curse and do not even realize it. And if their sole source of spiritual instruction is what their church leader tells them and they do not read the Holy Bible themselves so that they can personally take hold of and apply the promises and commands of God to their personal circumstances, their lives may be cut short.

Once again, you must understand that I am not saying that every infirmity is a direct result of the person's sin. Indeed the book of Job tells us that Job was afflicted with much pain and severe disease precisely because of his faith and obedience to God. The Bible tells us in the book of Job Chapter 1 that God called Job "blameless and upright" in Job's position towards God in his generation. And because Job was immensely blessed by God and protected by God with a hedge of protection as Job served God, satan had to get permission from God **before** he could break through to attack Job in Job's body. Satan accused Job of serving God only because of what Job could get from God and God used Job to prove satan wrong. Some things we may never understand this side of eternity as to why it is that some suffer affliction. After Job's test was over, God restored Job to health and Job lived one hundred and forty years and saw the children the Lord God gave him after Job's affliction and his children's children to the fourth generation. God rewarded Job with twice as much as Job had before Job's test of affliction.

God's original plan for mankind was for us to walk in health. God created Adam and Eve to live forever until their sin brought God's punishment of death and separation from God. What should you do if you are sick? We know from the actions of the Lord Jesus in the gospel of Matthew Chapter 12, verse 15 and the gospel of Luke Chapter 4, verse 40 that the Lord Jesus healed all who were ill and had various kinds of sicknesses. Anyone who came to the Lord Jesus for health in their physical body was healed by the Lord Jesus when they came to the Lord Jesus in faith or, as in the case of the man who was paralyzed, with the faith of their friends. There was no limit to the Lord Jesus' healing as we see in the gospel of Matthew Chapter 12, verse 15. Jesus did not say: "I have reached my quota for healing for the day." Why not? In 1st John Chapter 3, verse 8, we see that the Lord Jesus Christ came to destroy the works of the devil. The Lord Jesus is bigger than any challenge anyone can face and His power is greater than any curse.

If, perchance, you may be facing a challenge that seems insurmountable to you or if you feel you might be under a curse, DO NOT GIVE UP. If you are a born again believer and you are sick, the book of James Chapter 5, verse 14 in the Holy Bible says you should call for the elders of the church and have the elders anoint you with oil and pray the prayer of faith for you and the Lord Jesus will heal you, that is, raise you up. In verse 16 of the same chapter believers are told to confess their faults to one another and to pray for each other so that they may be healed. In other words, the Bible is saying that disobeying God's command to forgive those who have offended a person can lead to physical disease.

In the account of Jonah being swallowed by a big fish in the book of Jonah Chapter 1, verse 17 we see the result of disobedience to a personal command by God. In the book of Jonah Chapter 1, verse 1, God told Jonah to go to Nineveh and warn the people of Nineveh of God's judgment because of their wickedness. Well, Jonah was not too enthusiastic about that command because Jonah knew that if he preached to the people of Nineveh and the people repented from their sins and turned to God, God would not destroy Nineveh. Jonah wanted the people of Nineveh destroyed. Look at what happened. When Jonah was in the boat trying to run away from God's command, the people in the boat with Jonah began to sink. That was the result of God's punishment on Jonah because of Jonah's disobedience. Even when Jonah explained to them that he was the cause of the ship's problem they tried to find other ways to prevent the ship from sinking until they failed and realized they would sink with Jonah unless they threw Jonah overboard. When they threw Jonah off their ship, the ship's problem stopped. That is what I meant by not wanting to be a part of any curse by association. Church leaders and the congregations they minister to are in a "precarious" position if the leader turns his or her eyes off the Lord Jesus Christ. A whole congregation could be cursed. If the Bible clearly states God's position on an issue, whatever the issue of the day may be, and a people or nation chooses to disobey God, they not only sin against God and their own bodies, they may bring about certain curses on themselves and others connected to them. God wants us to be in the know so that we will place ourselves in position to receive God's blessings through the Lord Jesus Christ. All sin is sin and all sin can be forgiven by the Lord Jesus Christ when a person truly repents and asks for forgiveness from God. The mercies of God still hold true today. When a person anointed by the power of the Holy Spirit speaks in the power of the Name of Jesus to break a curse and to cast out an evil spirit, satan must comply and curses will be broken. It is important to remember the words of the Lord Jesus Christ when he said in the gospel of Matthew Chapter 17 that some evil spirits require prayer and fasting to be cast out. We see, therefore, that knowledge of God's Word is extremely important. If satan can keep a person ignorant then he can keep them in bondage. Even in the natural realm, what a person may not know may cause them to make wrong choices or decisions that will negatively impact them. In the United States we recently witnessed an example of this when the "Affordable Health Care Act" law was enacted. A Senator told her colleagues that they had to first pass that law and then find out what that law entailed and so that law was passed. The electorate was promised individuals could keep their current health plan if they liked it. The majority of the citizens believed those words and did not check to see what was written in that law. At election time the electorate had two choices; vote for a candidate who would retain that law or vote for a candidate who would repeal that law; the electorate chose the candidate who would retain that law. With the implementation of that law, millions will be dropped from the individual health insurance they thought they would keep because it does not comply with the new law. Many will complain about the new health care law and its enforcement. Changes will have to be made to the law. That is easier than accepting responsibility for not taking time to fully understand that law and its impact on their lives before going to the voting booth. Ignorance concerning the law will not protect them from being adversely affected by the law. Satan does not want you as a born again believer to know the full extent of your authority in the Lord Jesus because that would be destructive to satan's kingdom.

God wants you to know your rights in the Lord Jesus Christ and not just to know them, but to ENFORCE them. Some may place a negative connotation on the word 'rights' because they associate that word with entitlements and may have been taught that entitlements are wrong. We must not allow satan to try to manipulate what God has called 'good' into something that is considered evil. In the book of Hebrews Chapter 4, verse 16, we are encouraged to come **boldly** to God's throne. Why? It is because God has qualified us through the Lord Jesus Christ to be a part of God's family. With that comes the right to approach God's throne. A child has a right to be welcomed into his or her home and to expect his or her parents to make provision for the child's needs. And so the Lord Jesus says in Matthew Chapter 7, verse 11: "If you, then, though you are evil, know how to give good gifts to your children, how much more will your Father in heaven give good gifts to those who ask him!"

Write, Write,

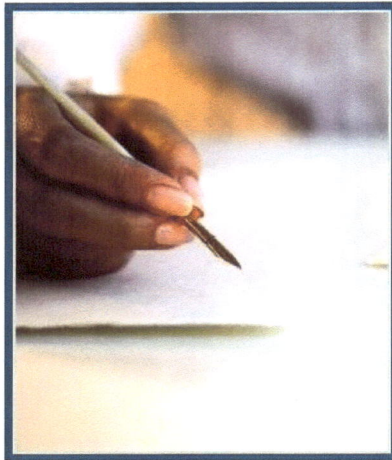

Keep on Writing…

THE POWER OF WORDS

This is one of the most important sections of this book. In the book of Proverbs Chapter 6, verse 2, we see an example of a person who has been trapped or ensnared by the words they spoke. In other words, people get themselves entangled or fall in a trap because of the **power** of words. One of the myths that many were taught growing up was that sticks and stones may break their bones but words would never hurt them. As so many grew up failing to recognize the power of words. Consider this. In the book of Genesis Chapter 1 we read that the earth in which we live was initially without form or void. God wanted to change that and what did God do? **The Lord God spoke WORDS**. In Genesis Chapter 1, verse 3 we read: "And God said "Let there be Light" and there was light." That is profound. <u>God created something just by the words that He spoke. In Genesis Chapter 1, verse 26 we are told that God created man in the image of God. That meant that man had the power to bring things into manifestation by the words that man spoke, just as God did.</u> In the book of Genesis, we see that whatever name Adam called an animal became the name of that animal. We are still using those names today. The name Adam gave to his wife, Eve, became her name and she is still spoken of as Eve to this day. **The question for us then becomes: How are you calling it, whatever the "it" in your life may be?**

With this understanding, let us look at some of the ways many are unknowingly cursed, especially some Bible believing Christians. Several years ago I attended a church where the Pastor would ask the congregation to say at the beginning of the sermon something like this: "Today is the best day of my life." At the time we would say that with gusto. But when I began to realize and see the results of the power of words I realized that the Pastor had unknowingly cursed the congregation. Why? That was because if "Today" was the best day of their lives, then everything that happened in their lives after that day would be downhill.

You have to understand that when the Lord Jesus cursed the fig tree when he did not find the fruit he was looking for, the fig tree did not die immediately. What happened was that the life to that fig tree was cut off but it took the branches and the leaves some time to show the effects of the words of the Lord Jesus Christ. The roots of the fig tree died with the curse and could no longer provide nourishment for the tree and so with time the tree shriveled up. It looked green and leafy one day and the next day the fig tree was dry and shriveled up. And that is what is happening in many congregations. The effects of the curses of the Pastor are not always immediately noticeable and things seem to be the same or even better for a short while. Then suddenly, people start losing their jobs, for example, or a hurricane comes through town and some lose practically all they had and have to rebuild from scratch. And they never make the connection between the words that were spoken, knowingly or unknowingly, against them and what is happening to them.

Just as important, and probably more so, are the words you speak to yourself. You see, the Pastor may speak to you once or twice a week but you talk to yourself every day. What are you saying to yourself? Have you heard people say things like nothing good ever happens to them and then wonder why so many things are going wrong in their lives. Or something bad happens to them and they may say things like "it comes in threes" and then two more bad things happen to them.

Another example is the use of the word "Blimey" in the course of some conversations. It is a common English expression which I found out means "Blind me!" or "God blind me!" And yet many who may inadvertently speak negatively may think they are just using a contemporary figure of expression.

Have you ever heard people ask why bad things sometimes happen to good people? This may be one of the reasons: The power of words spoken by them, over them, or to them, whether seriously or jokingly.

In Isaiah Chapter 42, verses 22 and 23, in the King James translation, it says: "But this is a people robbed and spoiled; they are all of them snared in holes, and they are hid in prison houses: they are for a prey, and none delivereth; for a spoil, and none saith, Restore. Who among you will give ear to this? who will hearken and hear for the time to come?" If something happens that should not be so, something that is clearly outside the will of God, it is okay to pray for God's reversal and restoration. So how do you know whether to agree or disagree with what is happening? You have to spend time with God. In the book of 1st Samuel Chapter 16, verse 1 God asked the prophet Samuel how long he was going to mourn for King Saul since God had rejected King Saul from being king. Yes, there was a time God had the prophet Samuel anoint Saul to be King. But when

Saul disobeyed God and consulted those who practiced evil, God rejected King Saul. It was understandable for the prophet Samuel to wish that King Saul had done better but God expected the prophet Samuel to move on to the next assignment God had for him and that was to anoint David to be the next King. In the book of 1st Peter Chapter 5, verse 8, the devil or satan is described as a prowling lion seeking those whom he may devour or destroy. And one of the ways he does this is by having people knowingly or unknowingly snare themselves by the words that they speak. In so doing they give satan the "loophole" or entrance satan needs to try to cause havoc in their lives. As you read this book you may recollect several instances where you have spoken words to yourself that were not beneficial to you. Or you might recall curses others may have spoken over you such as: "You will never amount to anything." Is life over for you as a result of their words? No! There is hope. **There is a power so great that no words can curse it and it is the power of the Name of the Lord Jesus Christ.**

You can break the power of every curse that you or anyone else has spoken in your life by cancelling their words as well as all negative words spoken to or about you that are contrary to God's will in your life by your right words. You speak to cancel the effects and consequences of the wrong words spoken into your life by applying the Name of the Lord Jesus to those situations and cancelling those words and their effects permanently in the Name of Jesus Christ. Remember, if you are a born again believer of the Lord Jesus Christ you are a child of God and an authorized representative of our Lord and Savior Jesus Christ. The Lord Jesus said in the gospel of John Chapter 6, verse 63 that the words that he spoke were spirit and life. **In other words, the words Jesus spoke had the power in the spiritual realm of authority to bring about changes in the natural realm.** When the Lord Jesus Christ told a person to be healed, the sickness had to respond to the spiritual authority of the Lord Jesus Christ and the sick person was healed. The prophet Elijah knew the power of words. He spoke to the weather in the book of 1st Kings Chapter 17, verse 1 and we read: Now Elijah the Tishbite, from Tishbe in Gilead, said to Ahab, "As the Lord, the God of Israel, lives, whom I serve, **there will be neither dew nor rain in the next few years except at my word.**" Elijah declared that it would not rain and for three years it did not rain. And then Elijah spoke again and declared that it would rain and it rained.

I have found out in my personal life that the weather is one of the easiest things to control when spoken to in faith in the name of the Lord Jesus Christ. In God's power and in the Name of the Lord Jesus Christ, I have spoken to hurricanes and seen them turn around and spoken to the rain and seen it abate when I had to fulfill a particular assignment or errand. And yet how many have perished in some of these hurricanes because their sole source of reference for the behavior patterns of the weather was to turn to the weather channels. There is nothing wrong with taking into account what trained professionals have to say about a particular situation but at the end of the day we have to decide who will have the **<u>final</u>** word in our situation. If the weather channel's forecast says the weather will be bad and you do not want a different outcome dress and act accordingly. If you want a different outcome pray and speak to the situation. Remember the words of the Lord Jesus in the gospel of Matthew Chapter 17, verse 20: "Truly I tell you, if you have faith as small as a mustard seed, you can say to this mountain, 'Move from here to there,' and it will move. Nothing will be impossible for you." If you have a mountain like obstacle or situation, speak to the situation in faith. Was the Lord Jesus Christ lying in Matthew Chapter 17, verse 20? No, it is impossible for God to lie, so if the Lord Jesus tells you your words can move an inanimate object as heavy as a mountain you had better believe it. That means if you have an obstacle that is attempting to block God's revealed will to you in your personal Christian life you can speak to that obstacle and command that it be moved in the Name of the Lord Jesus Christ.

And if you need another born again Christian to help you in speaking to the mountains in your life ask them for help. The book of Deuteronomy Chapter 32, verse 30 asks; "How could one man chase a thousand, or two put ten thousand in flight, unless their Rock had sold them, unless the Lord had given them up?" In other words, this principle demonstrates the exponential power of words; one person can chase a thousand people and two can chase ten thousand people. <u>THERE IS A CUMULATIVE POWER OF WORDS.</u> Practice makes perfect and some things we will not have complete knowledge of on this side of eternity.

God does not expect you to put yourself in harm's way or to be presumptuous when you pray. If you are not absolutely confident in what you say or you do not have peace concerning your words, you should re-examine the issue at hand and <u>operate at the level of your faith.</u> God already knows your heart and you do not have to impress men. There were things that I prayed for and spoke to that God in His wisdom did not bring to pass and in many instances I later thanked God for not answering those particular prayers. For the Lord Jesus tells us in Matthew Chapter 7, verse 9 that God will not give us a stone when we ask for food. In other words, God will give us what will strengthen us and not what God knows is not in our best interest.

You must note that after you speak words to cancel any curses that may have been spoken over you, you must speak blessings into your life. In other words, don't just remove the darkness; shine the light of the Lord Jesus into your life, specifically in the areas in which you are facing a challenge. **And remember, the principle of the cumulative power of words applies to words of blessing also.** Speak God's blessings and the favor of God and man into your life and also into the lives of those dear to you. Bless your family, your school, your church, and those God impresses on you to bless. In the book of Galatians Chapter 6, verse 7 we read that God is not mocked and that whatsoever a man sows that will he reap.

The final say as to the result of the words we speak in the Name of Jesus Christ rests with God. We must also remember that we only have the authority God gives us through the Lord Jesus Christ and if a person's lifestyle is in direct contradiction to the Word of God, God is under no obligation to honor what they speak. This brings us to another important principle. It matters with whom you associate when it comes to seeing the results of your prayers. In the gospel of Mark Chapter 5, verses 22 to 42 we read the account of the Lord Jesus Christ raising up Jairus's daughter. It is noteworthy that before the Lord Jesus Christ spoke to the girl to receive the miracle of life, the Lord Jesus first sent away or put out the naysayers and the mockers. In other words, the Lord Jesus Christ sent the naysayers and the mockers out of the environment in which he was going to perform the miracle. Why? They had mocked and ridiculed the Lord Jesus' faith filled words that would prepare them for the miracle he was about to perform. The Lord Jesus did not want the doubt of the naysayers and mockers to pollute Jairus's faith.

Treat your faith in God as a precious commodity and do not allow anyone to despise you for believing in God, in his Son, the Lord Jesus Christ and in the promises God has given you.

In the gospel of Matthew Chapter 7, verse 6 the Lord Jesus again emphasizes this important principle when he tells us not to give what is holy to the dogs. In other words, do not share what is sacred or precious to you with those who will ridicule or make fun of you, your dreams or your aspirations. In the book of Genesis Chapter 37, verse 5 Joseph shared his dream with his brothers and his brothers hated Joseph so much after the dream that they wanted to kill him. Joseph's brothers settled on selling Joseph into slavery instead of killing Joseph as they had initially planned. That did not prevent the dream God gave Joseph from coming to pass. Would Joseph have experienced the fulfillment of God's dream if he had not shared it with his brothers? Absolutely! And possibly, in a shorter time and with less drama.

I used to think everybody would be happy when good things happened to me or when God spoke a wonderful word in my life. After all, I would greatly rejoice when God did good things in their lives. And so it came as a surprise to me to find out that some of these "friends" could not celebrate my successes. If your Pastor or church leader cannot celebrate the dream you know for sure God gave you, it means they cannot effectively pray for you concerning that dream. In the book of Amos Chapter 3, verse 3 we read: "Do two walk together unless they have agreed to do so?" If the dream is important enough to you, you do not want to share it with those who not only may try to cause you to have doubts about yourself or the dream, but who might even speak negative words or curses concerning your dream.

That being said, there is a difference between seeking wise counsel and indiscriminately sharing your dreams and goals with others.

If you plan to do something that another person has great experience in and is willing to give you good advice regarding your dream, it may be a good thing to share your dreams with them and get their input. They may be able to show you some mistakes to avoid and ways to accelerate your dream. It takes commitment to God's plans for your life, prayer and discernment by the Holy Spirit to know who to speak to, pray with and collaborate with in your life. The Holy Scriptures are a wonderful source of direction and you should always study the Bible. Pray and ask God to give you insight into what the Bible has to say on your aspirations and concerning the challenges or circumstances in your life. For as the prophet Moses says in the book of Deuteronomy Chapter 32 verses 46 to 48: " …Take to heart all the words I have solemnly declared to you this day, so that you may command your children to obey carefully all the words of this law (that is, the commands given by God). **They are not just idle words for you - they are your life. By them you will live long in the land you are crossing the Jordan to possess.**"

Write, Write,

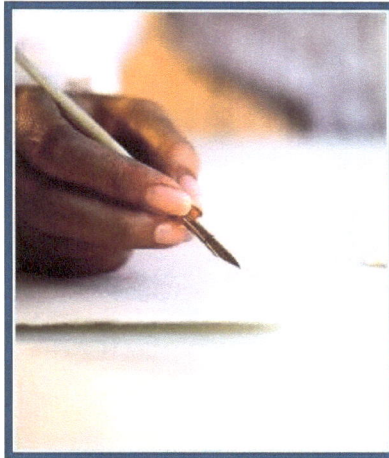

Keep on Writing…

THE CURSE OF AGREEMENT

This is a great follow-up to the previous chapter. The title itself seems to be an oxymoron. We have been taught to consider the word "agreement" to be a good thing and for the most part it is. We sign agreements with different groups or companies to perform or receive certain services. Indeed there is a peace of mind that comes from knowing what has been spelled out in a contract or written agreement. Agreements in writing can prevent confusion or misunderstanding as to what is expected of either party involved in the agreement. So, how can agreements become a curse?

In Christian circles the word "Amen" means "So be it" or "Let it be so". In many church sermons that is where the curse of agreement begins. "How so?" you might ask. It is with the indiscriminate use of the word "Amen". You see, some Pastors and church leaders repeat the word "Amen" after every few words or sentences mainly as a habit. It is a word they have a habit of saying in the course of their preaching. For example, the pastor may say something like this: "So your child is on drugs, Amen, the Lord can rescue them." For you, that would be true if your child is on drugs. But when the Pastor says "Amen", many in the congregation respond with the word "Amen". In other words, what they have just said is "Let it be so". If their child was not on drugs, they have just pronounced the curse of drugs on them. If the Pastor gives an example that affects you and you need agreement with that, then say "Amen" if that is what God needs to do for you. If not, recognize that particular sentence is not specifically for you and hold your Amen for when you need it. The Pastor may be saying "Amen" after every three or four words and may be oblivious to the fact that those agreeing with him or her may not be saying "Amen" in their best interest. That does not mean that you should not be attentive to what is being said. That is why the Lord Jesus Christ tells us in the King James translation of the gospel of Mark Chapter 4, verse 24: "… Take **heed what ye hear**: with what measure ye mete, it shall be measured to you: and unto you that hear shall more be given."

The curse of agreement extends in the lives of many beyond the walls of a church. You may have a conversation with someone that goes something like this: You know how it is when you grow old and you can't think right. And without giving it any further thought you say: "Yes". What did you just do? You have agreed to not thinking right when you grow old. Is that really what you want to happen to you? The Bible tells us in the book of Deuteronomy Chapter 34, verse 7, that the prophet Moses was one hundred and twenty years old and healthy. In the book of Joshua Chapter 14, verses 6 through 13, we read that Caleb was eighty-five years old when he asked for the land he had been promised. It reads: "Now the people of Judah approached Joshua at Gilgal, and Caleb son of Jephunneh the Kenizzite said to him, "You know what the Lord said to Moses the man of God at Kadesh Barnea about you and me. I was forty years old when Moses the servant of the Lord sent me from Kadesh Barnea to explore the land. And I brought him back a report according to my convictions, but my fellow Israelites who went up with me made the hearts of the people melt in fear. I, however, followed the Lord my God wholeheartedly. So on that day Moses swore to me, 'The land on which your feet have walked will be your inheritance and that of your children forever, because you have followed the Lord my God wholeheartedly.' "Now then, just as the Lord promised, he has kept me alive for forty-five years since the time he said this to Moses, while Israel moved about in the wilderness. So here I am today, eighty-five years old! I am still as strong today as the day Moses sent me out; I'm just as vigorous to go out to battle now as I was then. Now give me this hill country that the Lord promised me that day. You yourself heard then that the Anakites were there and their cities were large and fortified, but, the Lord helping me, I will drive them out just as he said." Then Joshua blessed Caleb son of Jephunneh and gave him Hebron as his inheritance." At the time Caleb was speaking in this passage it was forty five years later. Imagine, a whole generation later Caleb said he was just as strong then as he was when he was given the promise. <u>Caleb did not resign himself to someone else's opinion of what he should do at his age and neither should you.</u>

If your friend makes a statement about you that you disagree with, you could be polite and respond by saying: "I would hope not." That might probably startle them into thinking some more about what you just said and could be the start of a conversation that could be beneficial for both of you; one in which you both decide to encourage each other in a positive way. That way, instead of cursing each other you begin to bless each other.

What God is asking us to do is to have God's higher way of thinking. In the book of Isaiah Chapter 55, verse 9, God tells us that his thoughts are higher than our thoughts and his plans higher than our plans. In the book of Romans Chapter

12, verse 2, we are asked to renew our mind and thereby be transformed in order to bring about God's good, acceptable and perfect plan in our lives. We must not conform to nor be molded by the mindset of the world when that is in conflict with what God says. Will adjusting to God's way of thinking take time? Of course! And will we make mistakes along the way? As long as we are human beings on this earth, we will. But remember, that is why the Lord Jesus Christ came. Jesus came to die for ALL of our sins; sins of commission and omission, sins of words that have been wrongly spoken, and to break curses and oppression in any form. Meditate on what the Lord Jesus said in the book of Isaiah Chapter 61, verses 1 and 2, when he said: "The Spirit of the Sovereign Lord is on me, because the Lord has anointed me to proclaim good news to the poor. He has sent me to bind up the brokenhearted, to proclaim freedom for the captives and release from darkness for the prisoners, to proclaim the year of the Lord's favor..." If we say the wrong words we can repent of our wrong words and ask God to forgive us through Jesus Christ. And in the Name of the Lord Jesus we can break the curses that others may have spoken against us or that we might unknowingly have spoken against ourselves and replace them with faith filled good words about ourselves and about our circumstances.

We must also teach our children early in life to be selective as to whom they agree to hang out or socialize with. In the book of Proverbs Chapter 1, verse 10, Solomon instructs his son with these words: "My son, if sinful men entice you, do not give in to them." In the book of Proverbs Chapter 22, verse 6, we read: "Start children off on the way they should go, and even when they are old they will not turn from it." In other words, we are encouraged to bring up a child in the right way. What is the right way to bring up a child? It is to teach them the way of salvation through the Lord Jesus and to train them according to the commands and principles God gives us in the Holy Bible. It is especially important to be careful about the words you speak to your children when they are misbehaving. Do not curse them by saying they will never be successful in anything. And when you are joking do not say negative things about to your child such as "here comes trouble!" It will take time and practice to say the right words but thank God for the power of the blood of Jesus to forgive our wrong words when we confess them before God and to break any curses we may have inadvertently spoken.

As living examples, wherever we may be, we should let others see the power of the good agreements we make. Let us refuse to enter into agreements with words or principles contrary to the Word of God.

Write, Write,

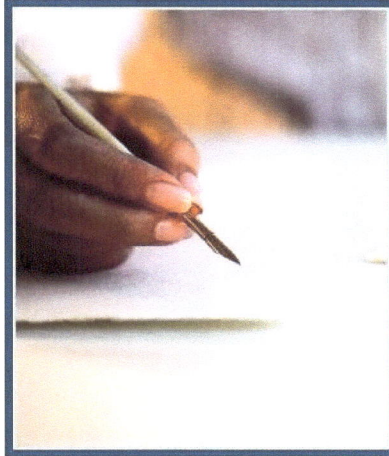

Keep on Writing…

THE CURSE OF INDIFFERENCE

In the book of Matthew Chapter 25 the Lord Jesus Christ gives us some insight as to how He will judge the deeds of men. It reads in verses 31 to 46: "When the Son of Man comes in his glory, and all the angels with him, he will sit on his glorious throne. All the nations will be gathered before him, and he will separate the people one from another as a shepherd separates the sheep from the goats. He will put the sheep on his right and the goats on his left. Then the King will say to those on his right, 'Come, you who are blessed by my Father; take your inheritance, the kingdom prepared for you since the creation of the world. For I was hungry and you gave me something to eat, I was thirsty and you gave me something to drink, I was a stranger and you invited me in, I needed clothes and you clothed me, I was sick and you looked after me, I was in prison and you came to visit me.' "Then the righteous will answer him, 'Lord, when did we see you hungry and feed you, or thirsty and give you something to drink? When did we see you a stranger and invite you in, or needing clothes and clothe you? When did we see you sick or in prison and go to visit you?' The King will reply, 'Truly I tell you, whatever you did for one of the least of these brothers and sisters of mine, you did for me.' **"Then he will say to those on his left, 'Depart from me, you who are <u>cursed,</u> into the eternal fire prepared for the devil and his angels. For I was hungry and you gave me nothing to eat, I was thirsty and you gave me nothing to drink, I was a stranger and you did not invite me in, I needed clothes and you did not clothe me, I was sick and in prison and you did not look after me.' They also will answer, 'Lord, when did we see you hungry or thirsty or a stranger or needing clothes or sick or in prison, and did not help you?' He will reply, 'Truly I tell you, whatever you did not do for one of the least of these, you did not do for me." Then they will go away to eternal punishment, but the righteous to eternal life."**

<u>The Lord Jesus Christ will judge the deeds of all people, taking into account what they did or did not do to help humanity. In this Chapter Jesus chastised those who did nothing when they saw the needs of others.</u>

This is not just applicable at the individual level it is also applicable at the corporate or church level. In a "give me, give me" society, for some it is all about advancing themselves at the expense of everyone else. Let us take the problem of hunger, a problem that faces many, not only in the United States of America, but all over the world. Why is it that some celebrities such as U2's Bono are working hard to eradicate world hunger and some Christians are doing nothing? True, you do not want a person to live their entire life dependent on someone else for food, especially if they have the capacity to work. However, hunger is not always attributable to laziness. **What can you do to empower another person and help them become self-sufficient in their area of need?**

Consider the problem of properly educating underprivileged children. Oprah Winfrey is spending thousands of dollars of her own money to fund the education of underprivileged children in Africa and some Christians will not even give a word of advice to a child who desperately needs their help. I was at the transit hub and heard an older woman start a conversation with a young African-American man. She asked him where he worked and he mentioned the local Amazon Company. It turned out he was getting off a long shift and he was obviously tired. The woman told how she had worked there as a seasonal worker during the Christmas holidays in order to make extra money to buy Christmas presents for her children. She then went on to say how she hated the work there and kept going on and on about how horrible the company was. Never mind the fact that the Amazon Company was offering employment with good pay to several African-American employees. The young man listened patiently. And she continued her rant for several more minutes. Finally he had had enough! The young man looked at her and said to her in exasperation: "You are supposed to encourage me!" He then went on to explain to her why her words to him were out of place. A pained expression came over her face as she realized what she had done. She was old enough to be his mother. She had not commented on his good work ethic. She had not encouraged him by giving him examples of how hard work had paid off for many who used the work ethics they gained from their earlier years. She did not tell him how pleased we should all be that he was making an honest living. There were so many words she could have said to make a positive contribution to that young man's life and she had let that opportunity slip by. Thank God for that young man who did not let her negative words ruin his job opportunity. It is easy to criticize without offering any solutions or taking any action to correct or alleviate the problem. Even worse, some criticize those, such as faith based and charter schools, who are actually trying to make a long term positive difference in the education of a child. My fellow believers, just saying words like "Children these days are so … and so …" and using negative words to describe them will not excuse you in the day that God demands answers. For the Lord Jesus Christ says in the book of Matthew Chapter 12, verses 36 and 37: "But I tell you that everyone will have to give account on the

Day of Judgment for every empty word they have spoken. For by your words you will be acquitted, and by your words you will be condemned." When I hear someone make a negative sweeping statement about all children I immediately ask them: "Is your child like that?" and their quick reply is: "No". **It is easy to give excuses when you know you should take action in a particular situation but do not want to take on the responsibility of doing what is needed to change the situation, especially if it demands your immediate attention.**

You might ask: You mean that God is concerned about whether people are treated justly or fairly? Seriously, Yes! God is so concerned that God allows people to go through severe and sometimes tragic experiences when they had thought they were getting way with injustice. In the book of Isaiah Chapter 58, verses 6 to 8, we read: "Is not this the kind of fasting I have chosen: to loose the chains of injustice and untie the cords of the yoke, to set the oppressed free and break every yoke? Is it not to share your food with the hungry and to provide the poor wanderer with shelter - when you see the naked, to clothe them, and not to turn away from your own flesh and blood? Then your light will break forth like the dawn, and your healing will quickly appear; then your righteousness will go before you, and the glory of the Lord will be your rear guard. Then you will call, and the Lord will answer; you will cry for help, and he will say: Here am I." Could it be that some are sick or do not have their prayers answered because of the way they treat the poor or because of their indifference to the plight of those unjustly treated?

In the midst of injustice it is refreshing to see inspiring examples in the lives of some who took a stand to right a wrong. President Nelson Mandela was a man who spoke up against the unjust regime of apartheid. It seemed at the time he was foolish in doing so, spending twenty-seven years in jail while others seemed to be getting away with the injustice of that society. But God was with Mr. Nelson Mandela and after he was released from prison he went on to become the President of a democratic South Africa. Today apartheid is no longer present; indeed some do not even know what apartheid means. The country of South Africa and indeed the world has been impacted by one man's decision to seek the common good of his fellow men, women and children. And yet it took much more than President Nelson Mandela to bring about change in South Africa. There were boycotts organized against companies, such as the petroleum oil companies, that did business in South Africa and there were protests demanding President Mandela's release. Was it easy? No. Did it look hopeless at times? Yes. But in the end a positive difference was made in the world.

In our daily affairs we are exposed to different circumstances. You may see something that needs to be done but is not getting done. Perhaps, someone needs a ride to work every day because he or she does not have a car. Do you gossip about the person, or do you raise funds to help purchase a car for the person? President Jimmy Carter saw the need for affordable housing and started Habitat for Humanity where people could invest sweat equity in lieu of money towards the purchase of their home. One of the women who worked at a local Community Center got her first home this way. At the time she was already a grandmother and you should have seen the joy that home brought her. She now had a home she owned where her children and grandchildren could come to visit and to stay. For her, that was priceless! What are **you** going to do to make a difference?

Just as there is a curse for those who do nothing when the situation confronting a person or community demands attention, so also there are rewards for doing the right thing for a person or persons, especially when the recipients may not otherwise be able to do so. In the book of Proverbs Chapter 19, verse 17, we read: "Whoever is kind to the poor lends to the LORD, and he will repay them for what they have done." Are you going to solve ALL the problems of your community? No! But when you have your priorities in order; God first, your family, and that includes you next, and then your community, God will direct you as to what you need to do, when you need to do it and where you need to act in order to make a difference in this world. Your rewards may not always be apparent on this earth, especially since you might not do work in areas of high visibility and might not need to publicize your good deeds. Remember, God takes note and since our rewards ultimately come from God, they are in God's time and of God's choosing.

A note of caution: God is looking at the sum total of a person's experience. A person cannot be a terrible person at home, beating up their spouse and children, and then organize the community soup kitchen and expect God to bless them. Their service will be of benefit to those using the services they are providing but does anyone want to miss out on his or her intended blessing because they were not living right? Remember what we discussed at the beginning of this book; **through the Lord Jesus Christ you have authority over the territory God has assigned to you. Use it!**

Write, Write,

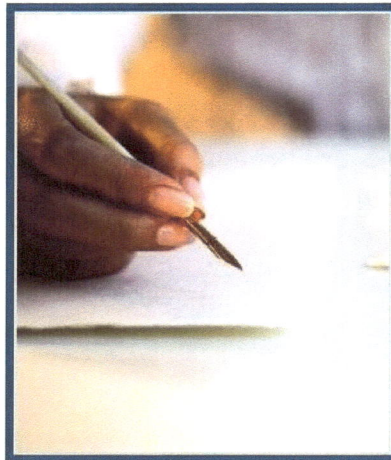

Keep on Writing…

THE CURSE OF DISPLACEMENT

"Where are you?" These are the famous words God asked Adam in the book of Genesis Chapter 3, verse 9. Adam had sinned by disobeying God. It was not that God did not know where Adam was. It was because Adam was not in his proper place. In verse 8 of the same Chapter it reads: "Then the man and his wife heard the sound of the Lord God as he was walking in the garden in the cool of the day, and they hid from the Lord God among the trees of the garden." God would visit Adam and Eve in the cool of the day and they would share times of fellowship but this time it was different. Adam had disobeyed God's command and responded in fear. Adam began to blame Eve for his actions and then blamed God for providing him with Eve. Eve began to blame the devil for her disobedience to God and that blame game continues with many today. How many times have you heard someone say the devil made them take a specific action that was contrary to the will of God?

As we examine this sequence of events, God has several important lessons for us. The first, and maybe the most obvious, is that God has a specific place for us. This is not being overly spiritual. God placed Adam in the garden. And when Adam met Eve, the garden was already present. The first place God placed you was in the home in which you were born. God chose your parents, you did not. And God chose the country of your birth. So let us start with an example using the home. If a child was three years old and somehow sneaked outside the kitchen door of the home and ran straight into the woods that child would not be in proper placement because the child would be outside his or her home. I know some of you might be asking why the parents chose to live so close to the woods in the first place but we will not discuss their personal preferences here so work with me. What could happen to a three year old who strayed from home and got lost in the woods? The child might become confused and frightened. The child might begin to cry. Being in the wrong place, outside the security of the home, could expose the child to danger. The child could potentially become a target for someone who had bad motives and could possibly cause harm to the child. The child might even wander into some animal's territory and get hurt or experience more problems. All of those possible harmful scenarios could result from something as simple as not being in the proper place! **In other words, being in the proper place gave the child the assurance of protection.**

We know that in a flawed world, the home which is supposed to be a child's place of safety may not always be so, but God designed the home to be a safe haven for all children. In the example above, being at the wrong place exposed the child to possible danger. In the book of Revelation Chapter 1, we see that Jesus Christ sent out specific words through John, his disciple, to the seven churches in the province of Asia. We note in the second and third book of Revelation that the Lord Jesus Christ knew the exact placement of these churches. He addressed the churches at Ephesus, Smyrna, Pergamum, Thyatira, Sardis, Philadelphia and Laodicea. The Lord Jesus noted the different attributes of each of these churches. In other words, for each church fellowship in the earth today there are unique attributes and qualities. Every person is a unique being and people generally tend to associate with those with whom they have much in common. When we decide to choose a local church congregation to fellowship with on a regular basis we must do so with God's guidance and direction. God has gifted each of us with different abilities, gifts and talents that are to be used in the service of God and mankind, all for the glory of God.

In the gospel of Matthew Chapter 13, we read of the different types of soil in which a farmer planted seed and how the different types of soil affected the seed that was planted in them. **In other words, you need the right environment for your gifts and talents to flourish.** Why is it that some schools produce better equipped students than others when it comes to the chances of their students attending a good college? In many cases, it is because they offer the right environment. Their school curriculum might be similar to that of competing schools but their school mission and vision, teachers, school code and extra curriculum activities may give their students an advantage over the others.

We have many decisions to make in life. Some decisions were made by our parents on our behalf when we were children but as we get older we assume more responsibility for the decisions that directly affect or have an impact on us. We must decide where we will attend college, live, work, raise our children, attend church and so forth. At first thought, it would easy to just continue things in the same tradition we have been brought up. For example, our family always attended this college and so we might decide to attend their alma mater and there is nothing necessarily wrong with that. Maybe your family has always fellowshipped with a particular church congregation. Again, there is nothing necessarily wrong with that. At times our choices may be influenced by something as simple as a routine to which we have become accustomed that may have outlived its usefulness. For example, a person may have been working at a particular company for forty-seven years. And again, there is nothing necessarily wrong with that. In fact, it says a lot to your commitment to the company to have worked there for so long. **The question we must ask when faced with decisions we have to make is whether the decision or choice we are about to make will <u>help</u> us reach our greatest potential in and with God in that arena.** You might respond by saying something like: "Oh, I am not looking to be famous" or "I am not looking to make a lot of money", but that may be an excuse to avoid the responsibility of doing something great with your life. The question then becomes: "How do we define greatness?" The Lord Jesus Christ gave us the answer in the gospel of Matthew Chapter 20, verses 25 and 26, and it reads: "Jesus called them together and said, "You know that the rulers of the Gentiles lord it over them, and their high officials exercise authority over them. Not so with you. Instead, whoever wants to become great among you must be your servant." Jesus Christ demonstrated this when he left heaven to come and live on this earth. Jesus served on this earth in many capacities and demonstrated an example of his servitude visually by washing the feet of his disciples. And then Jesus gave his life in the greatest service to humanity; our redemption from sin.

In order to most effectively serve others, you must be at your maximum potential in whatever area or endeavor you undertake. And it starts with knowing who you are and having a plan for Success. In the book of Judges Chapter 9, verses 7 to 15, Jotham gave the people of Shechem this interesting parable. It reads: "When Jotham was told about this, he climbed up on the top of Mount Gerizim and shouted to them, "Listen to me, citizens of Shechem, so that God may listen to you. One day the trees went out to anoint a king for themselves. They said to the olive tree, 'Be our king.' But the olive tree answered, 'Should I give up my oil, by which both gods and humans are honored, to hold sway over the trees?' Next, the trees said to the fig tree, 'Come and be our king.' But the fig tree replied, 'Should I give up my fruit, so good and sweet, to hold sway over the trees?' Then the trees said to the vine, 'Come and be our king.' But the vine answered, 'Should I give up my wine, which cheers both gods and humans, to hold sway over the trees?' Finally all the trees said to the thornbush, 'Come and be our king.' The thornbush said to the trees, 'If you really want to anoint me king over you, come and take refuge in my shade; but if not, then let fire come out of the thornbush and consume the cedars of Lebanon!" The olive tree, the fig tree and the vine in this parable knew who they were and what their assignment from God was and they would not be detracted from God's mission, no matter how glamorous the temptation. The thornbush was insecure and was not sure if the people really wanted him to be king. He did not see himself as a king but was willing to do what the people asked if it would make him look good. But note the conditions. He would accept being their king but if they changed their mind he wanted fire to come out of him to consume the tall cedars of Lebanon.

Be wary of advice given by a person who does not understand their true identity or who will compromise their beliefs or assignments to please people instead of first pleasing God.

The Lord Jesus Christ knew who he was, who sent him and his purpose here on earth. In the gospel of John Chapter 1, John speaks of the Lord Jesus as the Son who came from the Father. Also in the gospel of John Chapter 12, verse 49 the Lord Jesus says that he speaks the words the Father who sent him commanded him to say. Listen to what he says about his purpose in the gospel of John Chapter 6, verses 38 and 39. It reads: "For I have come down from heaven not to do my will but to do the will of him who sent me. And this is the will of him who sent me, that I shall lose none of all those he has given me, but raise them up at the last day. For my Father's will is that everyone who looks to the Son and believes in him shall have eternal life, and I will raise them up at the last day."

But just as important as knowing who you are, is having a plan to carry out your assignment. The Lord Jesus in the gospel of Matthew Chapter 7 gives us the parable where he describes the wise and foolish builders. On the surface it looked like they had both accomplished the same thing, building a house. However, when the time of testing came, the structure of the foolish builder fell while that of the wise builder remained. And the Lord Jesus asks in the gospel of Luke Chapter 14, verse 28: "Suppose one of you wants to build a tower. Won't you first sit down and estimate the cost to see if you have enough money to complete it?" In other words, who would embark on a building project without factoring in the costs and everything else that has to go with that decision? Lest they begin the building and not have the funds or resources to complete it and the unfinished product become a testament to their lack of planning. Planning and proper placement are vitally important and help to ensure that by God's grace and power, what we do in our lifetime will stand the test of God's eternal purpose for mankind.

Write, Write,

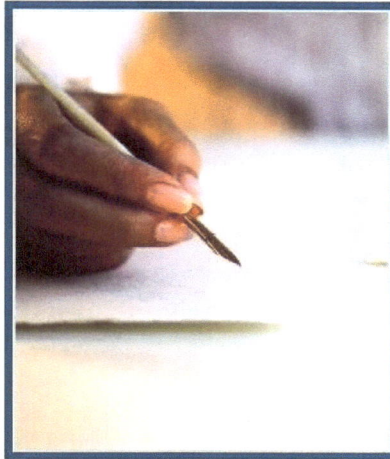

Keep on Writing…

EPILOGUE

We must apply the principles we have studied in this book. We have studied the power of Authority and Agreement, of doing what God says to do and of our Words. We have learned from the Scriptures the Curses of Arrogance, Disobedience, Indifference and Displacement. I pray that each of us will experience the totality of God's work in and through us for the glory of God. The Apostle Paul prayed in the book of Ephesians Chapter 3, verses 20 and 21: "Now to him who is able to do immeasurably more than all we ask or imagine, according to his power that is at work within us, to him be glory in the church and in Christ Jesus throughout all generations, for ever and ever! Amen." God has done His part in revealing the truths and principles of the Holy Bible to us. We have to respond by doing our part.

And so the question now asked of each one of us is this: "So what are you going to do?"

Write, Write,

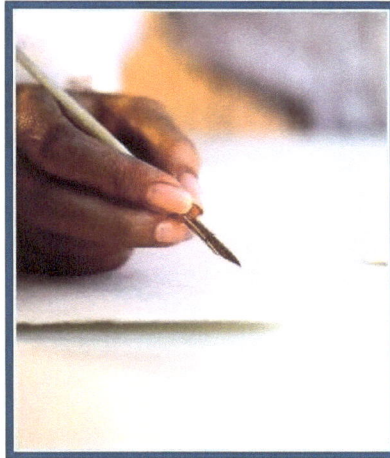

Keep on Writing…

"CALL TO ACTION" WORKSHEETS

The following "Call to Action" worksheets are meant to be a general guide. As you recall the lessons taught in each chapter, write down the areas in your life where you need to make changes and what you are going to do differently to bring about that change. They are not a substitute for professional or expert advice. For specific circumstances, please seek expert advice.

CALL TO ACTION: Authority - Who Has It?

1. Areas in my life I need to change:

_____
_____
_____
_____
_____
_____
_____
_____
_____
_____
_____
_____
_____
_____
_____
_____
_____
_____
_____
_____
_____
_____
_____
_____
_____
_____
_____
_____
_____
_____
_____
_____
_____

2. What I am going to do to bring about that change?

_____
_____
_____
_____
_____
_____
_____
_____
_____
_____
_____
_____
_____
_____
_____
_____
_____
_____
_____
_____
_____
_____
_____
_____
_____
_____
_____
_____
_____
_____
_____
_____
_____
_____
_____

CALL TO ACTION: The Curse of Arrogance

1. Areas in my life I need to change:

_____
_____
_____
_____
_____
_____
_____
_____
_____
_____
_____
_____
_____
_____
_____
_____
_____
_____
_____
_____
_____
_____
_____
_____
_____
_____
_____
_____
_____
_____
_____
_____

2. What I am going to do to bring about that change:

_____
_____
_____
_____
_____
_____
_____
_____
_____
_____
_____
_____
_____
_____
_____
_____
_____
_____
_____
_____
_____
_____
_____
_____
_____
_____
_____
_____
_____
_____
_____
_____
_____
_____

CALL TO ACTION: Do What God Says

1. Areas in my life I need to change:

_____
_____
_____
_____
_____
_____
_____
_____
_____
_____
_____
_____
_____
_____
_____
_____
_____
_____
_____
_____
_____
_____
_____
_____
_____
_____
_____
_____
_____
_____
_____

2. What I am going to do to bring about that change:

_____
_____
_____
_____
_____
_____
_____
_____
_____
_____
_____
_____
_____
_____
_____
_____
_____
_____
_____
_____
_____
_____
_____
_____
_____
_____
_____
_____
_____
_____
_____
_____
_____
_____
_____

CALL TO ACTION: The Curse of Disobedience

1. Areas in my life I need to change:

_____
_____
_____
_____
_____
_____
_____
_____
_____
_____
_____
_____
_____
_____
_____
_____
_____
_____
_____
_____
_____
_____
_____
_____
_____
_____
_____
_____
_____
_____

2. What I am going to do to bring about that change:

_____
_____
_____
_____
_____
_____
_____
_____
_____
_____
_____
_____
_____
_____
_____
_____
_____
_____
_____
_____
_____
_____
_____
_____
_____
_____
_____
_____
_____
_____
_____
_____
_____

CALL TO ACTION: The Power of Words

1. Areas in my life I need to change:

2. What I am going to do to bring about that change:

_____
_____
_____
_____
_____
_____
_____
_____
_____
_____
_____
_____
_____
_____
_____
_____
_____
_____
_____
_____
_____
_____
_____
_____
_____
_____
_____
_____
_____
_____
_____
_____
_____
_____
_____
_____

CALL TO ACTION: The Curse of Agreement

1. Areas in my life I need to change:

_____
_____
_____
_____
_____
_____
_____
_____
_____
_____
_____
_____
_____
_____
_____
_____
_____
_____
_____
_____
_____
_____
_____
_____
_____
_____
_____
_____
_____
_____
_____

2. What I am going to do to bring about that change:

_____
_____
_____
_____
_____
_____
_____
_____
_____
_____
_____
_____
_____
_____
_____
_____
_____
_____
_____
_____
_____
_____
_____
_____
_____
_____
_____
_____
_____
_____
_____
_____
_____

CALL TO ACTION: The Curse of Indifference

1. Areas in my life I need to change:

_____

_____

_____

_____

_____

_____

_____

_____

_____

_____

_____

_____

_____

_____

_____

_____

_____

_____

_____

_____

_____

_____

_____

_____

_____

2. What I am going to do to bring about that change:

_____
_____
_____
_____
_____
_____
_____
_____
_____
_____
_____
_____
_____
_____
_____
_____
_____
_____
_____
_____
_____
_____
_____
_____
_____
_____
_____
_____
_____
_____
_____
_____
_____
_____
_____
_____
_____
_____
_____
_____
_____
_____
_____
_____

CALL TO ACTION: The Curse of Displacement

1. Areas in my life I need to change:

_____
_____
_____
_____
_____
_____
_____
_____
_____
_____
_____
_____
_____
_____
_____
_____
_____
_____
_____
_____
_____
_____
_____
_____
_____
_____
_____
_____
_____
_____
_____
_____

2. What I am going to do to bring about that change:

_____
_____
_____
_____
_____
_____
_____
_____
_____
_____
_____
_____
_____
_____
_____
_____
_____
_____
_____
_____
_____
_____
_____
_____
_____
_____
_____
_____
_____
_____
_____
_____
_____

Write, Write,

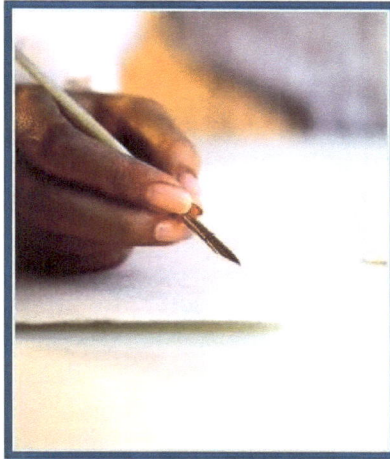

Keep on Writing…

MEET THE AUTHOR:

DR. SHEILA HAYFORD

Dr. Sheila Hayford is a retired Physician, Author and Publisher. After working at the Johns Hopkins Hospital in Maryland and the DuPont Hospital for Children in Delaware, she established and enjoyed her private Pediatric Practice. After twenty years in the medical field she retired from medicine to pursue her lifelong passion of reading and writing and to help others do the same.

Dr. Hayford is the author of numerous scientific articles, newspaper articles and medical columns for various journals. She has also authored and published several books including "Snatched from the Fire - One Man's Compelling Story", "Sailing into Destiny" and "God's Sound Bites." Dr. Hayford is also a Workshop Facilitator and Motivational Speaker and conducts Book Writing and Publishing Seminars.

As an extension of her passion to empower individuals and help them achieve their fullest potential, she serves as C.E.O. of The S.M.M.I.L.E. Foundation, an organization that focuses on supporting and mentoring men in the areas of Leadership and Entrepreneurship. If you would like Dr. Hayford to speak at your event, or would like information on hosting Dr. Hayford's Book Writing and Publishing Seminars and Workshops "ON LOCATION" at your church or organization, please send your request to info@whatawordpublishing.com

To request Speaking engagements, Radio and Television program engagements, or for more information about the S.M.M.I.L.E. Foundation, please email your requests to: info@whatawordpublishing.com

THE VISION; OUR MISSION:

What A Word Publishing and Media Group is pleased to do our part in promoting and enhancing Book Writing, Book Reading and Book Publishing worldwide. We believe that everyone has a story to tell; each story as varied as our life experiences. We believe that each story can have a positive benefit and, in some cases, a life changing effect on another person's life. We also recognize the barriers to book writing and publishing that may confront an individual. To this end we offer nationwide Book Writing Seminars and Hands-On Workshops. Our Book Seminars are designed to demystify the book writing and publishing process and our workshops are designed to provide hands-on experience in initiating the book writing process. We also offer Book Writing Seminars and Hands-On Workshops "ON LOCATION" so your group, church or organization's members can experience our book writing Seminars and Workshops at their location.

For those who would like more individualized attention, we provide private Book Coaching, Editing, Resume and Professional Services and work with varying schedules and budgets. Our goal is to bring the book writing and publishing dreams of many to reality. To request information on hosting a Book Seminar and Hands-On Workshop, or for private Book Coaching and other Professional Services, please visit the website or contact us via email at: info@whatawordpublishing.com

Visit us online at www.whatawordpublishing.com

Write, Write,

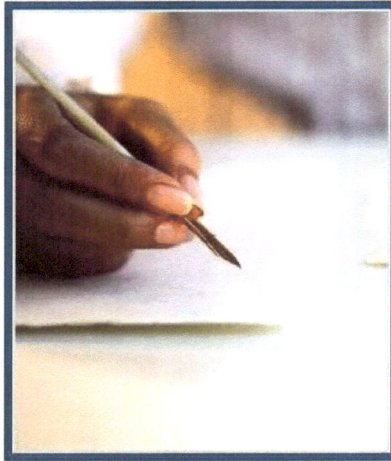

Keep on Writing…

STILL STANDING

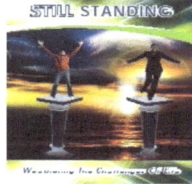

Email: info@whatawordpublishing.com

www.whatawordpublishing.com

The book "Still Standing" is a compilation of the stories of eight African-American individuals. It tells of the struggles and issues they faced, some originating in their teen years and persisting into adulthood, and how they overcame their challenges. This book is an easy read and excellent material for starting discussions on the challenges we face in life and learning from the experiences of others. Says Dr. Sheila Hayford, the author of several books including "Snatched from the Fire - One Man's Compelling Story" and "Sailing Into Destiny - The Providential Way": "What we do with our challenges is up to us. At the end of the challenge who will be left standing? Will the issue facing us have the upper hand or will we experience our victory?"

Still Standing is available is available in print and may be purchased online at http://www.whatawordpublishing.com   Share this book with your family and friends. We also hope you will share the book with your favorite book club. If you would like to experience our Book Writing and Publishing Seminars and Workshops "ON LOCATION" please send an e-mail to info@whatawordpublishing.com. We would be happy to send you our current titles as well as advance notification of our upcoming book titles when requested. We invite you to visit our website at http://www.whatawordpublishing.com

HAPPY READING!

PRESS RELEASE

NOW IN AUDIOBOOK: SAILING INTO DESTINY

Submitted by What A Word Publishing and Media Group

Email: info@whatawordpublishing.com

"Sailing Into Destiny" is now available in Audio book on Amazon and iTunes. We have had great reviews of the print and e-book versions and trust you will enjoy this format.

Book Excerpt: As the great vessel pulled away gently from the Canadian port of Seven Islands into the mighty ocean, George heard a voice speaking to him loud and clear: "This is the defining moment of the dream so prepare to launch out into the deep." This was only a fraction of the mega dream that George had envisioned years ago. The water was raging and boisterous, but they sailed slowly and majestically to their next port of call where the test of "desire and will" would be applied.

As always, we invite you to share this book with your family and friends. We also hope you will share the book with your favorite book club. If you would like to experience our Book Writing and Publishing Seminars and Workshops "ON LOCATION" please e-mail us at info@whatawordpublishing.com. We would be happy to send you our current titles as well as advance notification of our upcoming book titles when requested.

HAPPY READING!

AUDIOBOOK NOW AVAILBLE:

"DON'T LET THE PASTOR CURSE YOU"

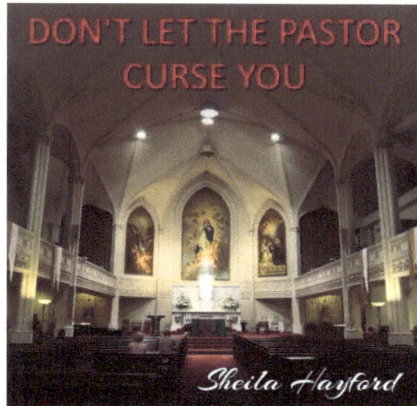

Announcing the release of this timely Audiobook, "Don't Let the Pastor Curse You." Far from being a Pastor bashing book, it is a thought provoking book written with passion. Recommended for general reading, it is also recommended for use in pastoral training worldwide. Available in print and e-book formats on www.amazon.com and in audiobook on www.audible.com or I-tunes.

A Must-Read and a Must Hear!

Great for gift giving!

Order yours today!

Book Excerpts: "This book is about Right Thinking, Right Speaking and Right Living … There are some things taking place within the church that are not necessarily within the will of God and in the process many are suffering under various curses. When faced with various challenges and tough circumstances, the natural inclination is to ask "Why?" In this book, God gives us an answer to some of the "Why?" questions. … And so the question becomes: Is it really possible to live a curse-free life? Read on!" ©Dr. Sheila Hayford, Author.

"The author explores various biblical themes with accuracy and passion. The reading includes a variety of illustrative Bible verses, as well as relatable author commentary readers can connect to. Chapter sizes are congruent to each other, creating a streamlined appearance in the text. Readers will find the content is well balanced. The conclusion creates a strong ending for the book that is concise and complete." Editorial Review

Submitted by: What A Word Publishing and Media Group.
http://www.whatawordpublishing.com

For more information send email to: info@whatawordpublishing.com

TO OUR READERS

We thank and appreciate you for reading this book. We encourage you to order additional copies to share with family and friends.

BOOK ORDERS

We invite you to order our published titles by visiting: www.whatawordpublishing.com, www.amazon.com or your favorite online retailer or bookstore. You may also order the audiobook "Don't Let The Pastor Curse You" by Dr. Sheila Hayford at www.audible.com or via I-Tunes.

Notes

Notes

Notes

Notes

Notes

Notes

Notes

Notes

Notes

Notes

Notes

Notes

Notes

www.ingramcontent.com/pod-product-compliance
Lightning Source LLC
Chambersburg PA
CBHW060804270326
41927CB00002B/44